WESTMINSTER ABBEY

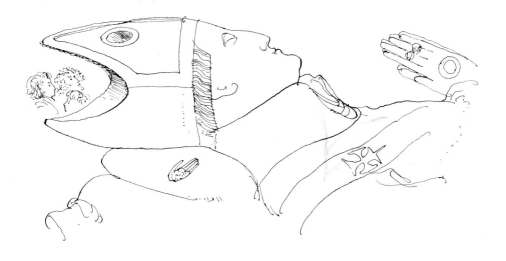

Simon de Langham, Abbot of Westminster, Bishop of Ely, Archbishop of Canterbury and Cardinal, was very talented, very wealthy and held the high office of Chancellor of England. He could be described as the third founder of the Abbey.

WESTMINSTER ABBEY

Edward Carpenter and David Gentleman

Merry Christmas 1993
To My Son Larry
Love Mom

Apt #1711 · 553 W. Cornelia Ave
Chicago, IL

Weidenfeld and Nicolson
London

The pictures on pages 15, 24, 25, 27, 32, 39, 47, 60, 64, 76, 82 and 123 were commissioned by the Abbey and erected as screens in the East Cloister during extented restoration work there. The endpaper pattern is derived from the incized decorative motif which appears on many flat surfaces in the Abbey Nave.

Text copyright © Edward Carpenter 1987
Illustrations copyright © David Gentleman 1987

Designed by Simon Bell

First published in Great Britain in 1987 by
George Weidenfeld & Nicholson Limited
91 Clapham High Street, London SW4 7TA

ISBN 0 297 79085 4

Illustration separations by Newsele Litho Ltd
Filmset by Keyspools Ltd, Golborne, Lancashire
Printed in Italy

Contents

	Foreword	6
	Plan of the Abbey	8
1	A Visit to the Abbey	9
2	Origins	18
3	Two Churches	22
4	'In Quires and Places where they Sing'	36
5	A Royal Peculiar	52
6	Community and College	56
7	'The Old Order Changeth Yielding Place to New'	70
8	Coronations	83
9	Monuments and Memorials	97
10	Two Nineteenth-Century Deans	110
11	'No Man is an Island Entire of It Self'	120
	Index	125

Foreword

Sɪʀ Rɪᴄʜᴀʀᴅ Sᴛᴇᴇʟᴇ paid a compliment to the charitable Lady Elizabeth Hastings in these words: 'To love her is a liberal education'. Those who have come to know Westminster Abbey over long years, and this applies to myself, do not hesitate to resort to such language in expressing their deep personal devotion to this great institution. This Collegiate Church has watched, been part of and recorded a stirring national history. To multitudes it has become the locus around which profound and subliminal emotions cluster, registering those thoughts which break through language and escape. Perhaps this is to be expected in a building which has been prayed in, rejoiced in, wept in by kings and commoners, saints and sinners over the centuries.

Such is Westminster Abbey for me and because of this I was excited when I heard that David Gentleman was drawing some fifty sketches in colour representing Westminster Abbey and its varied existence across the centuries. I have long admired his work, in which his imaginative flights of fancy wedded to a high technique combine to give life in a way which few photographs can hope to rival. David Gentleman's drawings invite, indeed constrain, the beholder to engage in the same creative apprehension as brought these fine pictures to birth. Thus when writing this portrait of the Abbey, I overcame the sense of inadequacy which I felt despite my ten years as Dean. I am sure that when my language falters and fails, David's drawings will take over, excite and interest.

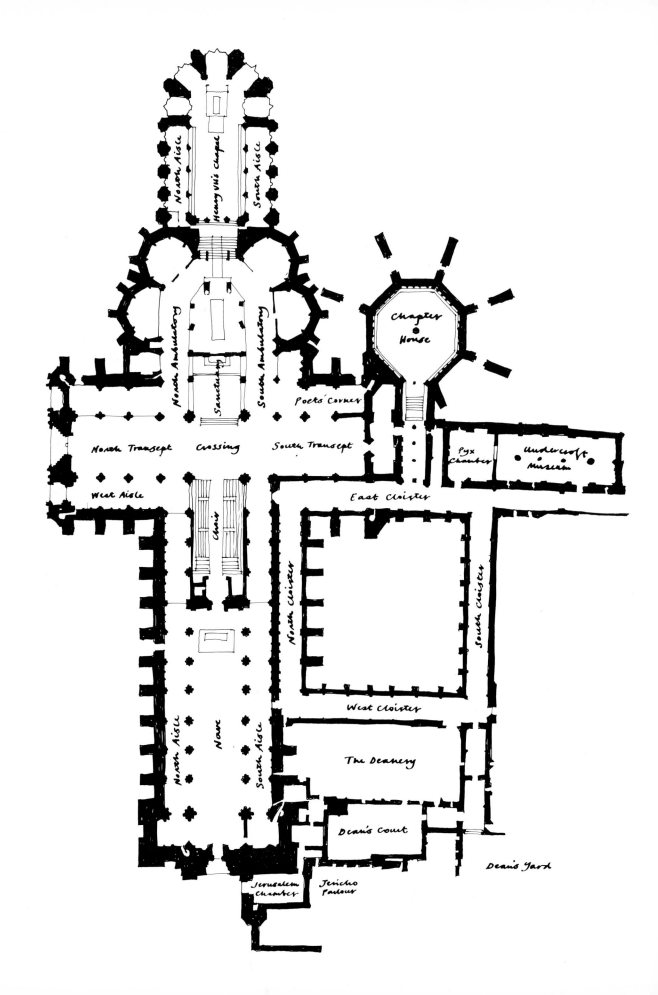

North Aisle

Henry VII's Chapel

South Aisle

North Ambulatory

Sanctuary

South Ambulatory

Poets' Corner

Chapter House

North Transept

Crossing

South Transept

Pyx Chamber

Undercroft Museum

West Aisle

East Cloister

Choir

North Cloister

South Cloister

West Cloister

The Deanery

North Aisle

Nave

South Aisle

Dean's Court

Dean's Yard

Jerusalem Chamber

Jericho Parlour

ONE

A Visit to the Abbey

Entry into Westminster Abbey is through the glass doors at the West End of the Nave or by the West Cloister. The splendid North Door, splendid both in its conception and execution, is no longer used because of the huge number of visitors to the Abbey – three and a half million people annually. It may seem paradoxical that because numbers are so high it is necessary to close a door which to the passer-by looks like a main entrance but this is due to the fact that inside, moving eastwards to Henry VII's Chapel, the Abbey becomes narrower. Hence, some years ago, a route beginning at the West End and having its exit in the East Cloister was instituted. In certain respects this is unfortunate, for W.H.Davies' words remain true even in a great Abbey: 'What is this life if, full of care, we have no time to stand and stare.' But standing and staring are possible during quieter moments of the day.

What will be your general impression on entering the Church? What impact does it make and what reaction does it provoke? I can answer this only too easily in respect of myself as I recall my first visit at the age of ten when I came up from the country with a party from our village school. Alas! it was an impression of sepulchral and unrelieved gloom. I am confident that this response is felt no longer, for a vast cleaning operation has taken place and the Abbey has been given a face lift. It is potentially a light and airy building, but when I first saw its interior it was black with the grime of centuries – and maybe a shellac which Sir Christopher Wren applied to the columns as a preservative. Sir Christopher would have done better – as happened in 1966 – to remove the dirt which in itself serves to corrode stone, preventing reflection of light and reducing detail and colour to a dull and flat uniformity.

Once inside the Abbey you will, I am sure, be constrained to peer upwards to the vaulted roof,

Plan of the Abbey.

white and resplendent with its golden bosses, some 102 feet above you. In imagination, you are transported to the German forests with their overhanging branches of which Gothic architecture may be a vestigial memory; or you may glimpse the hull of a great ship reminiscent of those pirate Northmen who roamed the seas to pillage and to plunder. As you lift your eyes to the majesty of the scene above, you feel yourself cut down to life size, a little boat on a vast sea. It is true that externally the Abbey has been dwarfed by the Victoria Tower and by a number of tall buildings, some of them veritable horrors, along Victoria Street. But these office blocks, so vast without, are pygmies from within.

Westminster Abbey, it must be admitted, was not built for utility. Its length and height were unnecessary for a small community of Benedictine monks to sing daily their *opus dei*. Such dimensions were to enable the spirit to soar with the building. Yet such is the paradox of the Abbey that as you experience its upward thrust so you are made aware of monuments galore of all shapes and sizes spanning diverse periods of history. Here are monuments to the good and bad, to those who have served God and his people well and others who have been content to serve themselves. Maybe this concentration of marble will remind you of this too too solid flesh; the hopes and fears that fallible men set their hearts upon; the kingdoms which mankind fitfully builds but which have no continuing stay – the glory of man and his shame. From this dilemma between what is and what ought to be, the Abbey, if it is true to itself, cannot escape.

One thing that the Abbey is unable to provide on an ordinary weekday, unless you penetrate to St Faith's Chapel at the south end of Poets' Corner, is quiet and the kind of positive stillness characteristic of a village church. Around you are many fellow human beings, men, women and children, from the four quarters of the globe, of different cultures and ethnic origins. This means, alas, noise. However, this is no new phenomenon.

The North Front Door, redesigned by Sir Gilbert Scott, a worthy entry into the Abbey, but seldom used.

The Crossing (RIGHT), specially commissioned by Henry III as a 'theatre for coronations'.

During the Middle Ages pilgrims would have crowded into the Nave, or the North Transept, *en route* for St Edward's Chapel and his Shrine. Also for over a century the Chapter House was used for the Lower House of Parliament which meant that knights from the shires and burghers from the towns were 'milling' around the church and Precincts, making it what a modern historian has described as the 'noisiest monastery in Western Europe'.

In the Nave of the Abbey is the grave of the Unknown Warrior. When I first came to Westminster I asked Mr Tom Hebron, the Receiver General, what began the influx of tourists into the Abbey at an ever-increasing rate. To my surprise, he replied without hesitation that it resulted from the unveiling of the Unknown Warrior's grave by King George V and his continued interest in it. It is true that for many unchurched people this has become a secular shrine almost vying with that of St Edward, King and Confessor. Maybe in 1918, when at long last all was quiet on the Western Front, there was an intuitive feeling, begotten of so great a tragedy, that life would never be the same again. Thus this grave has become a place of pilgrimage, a locus for the laying of wreaths by heads of foreign governments who might be embarrassed if they were to undertake this anywhere else in the Abbey. It demands of them nothing but compassion for the fallen and those who mourn along with some elemental commitment to 'never again'.

I can recall some fascinating reactions of eminent visitors to the Abbey. When I first came to this Collegiate Church I received Dr Adenauer, the aged German Chancellor, and escorted him round the building. When we came to the Crossing I pointed out to him, in the South Transept, the Poets' Corner and, in the North, the Statesmen's Aisle. 'Those people', he commented, pointing southwards, 'will get to Heaven long before those', pointing northwards. He thought for a moment and said: 'But then God is very mericiful.' Dr Adenauer had a personal interest in the Abbey since one of his sons was a Benedictine monk and he himself was hidden from the Nazis in a monastery.

It fell to me to receive the Russian leader Mikhail Gorbachov and to take him round the Abbey. I found that he was particularly curious as to why Charles Darwin, the famous author of that epoch-making work *The Origin of Species*, should have a memorial in a Christian church. I hope I gave him a satisfactory answer. On another, earlier occasion a leader of another Faith asked me blankly: 'What is that heretic doing in the Abbey?' When I referred to the singing of our Choir, Mr Gorbachov replied that there were fine choirs in the Russian Orthodox Church.

Beyond the Nave is the enclosed Choir. On the right is the stall that the Queen, Visitor of the Abbey, normally occupies when she attends a service. (She sometimes sits in the Sacrarium near the High Altar.) In the Choir – the stalls were designed by Edward Blore, Surveyor of the Fabric, in the mid-nineteenth century – are the seats for various officers of the Collegiate Church, including the Lord Mayor of Westminster who is Deputy High Steward, and the High Commissioners of the countries of the Commonwealth. The Dean and Chapter take a pride in having a close link with the member states of this association of sovereign states. Most of them have celebrated their independence by a service of Thanksgiving and Dedication in the Abbey. They continue to keep up the link, if they wish, by attending Evensong on their national day and also the annual Commonwealth Observance, at which the Queen, the Head of the Commonwealth, is present.

Ancient institutions tend to be excessively conservative and this can manifest itself in odd, though usually innocuous, ways. The Abbey is no exception. In a service some years ago all those seated in the upper stalls of the Choir were men. Why? The answer is simple. The Abbey started life as a Benedictine monastery and the monks occupied these stalls as they sang their daily offices. They were men! After many years the Dean and Chapter made the momentous decision that women should be admitted. Perhaps I ought to add that this was done before the Sex Discrimination Act was passed!

Proceeding eastwards you arrive at the Crossing which is part of the 'theatre' – that is the extensive open space now, alas, chaired, specially designed by Henry III for the staging of coronations – and the reason for the Choir being tucked away to the west. Once a year in preparation for the annual Judges' Service, the Nave is completely cleared and looks quite magnificent. The great supporting columns seem to grow out of the ground like gigantic trees soaring heavenwards. The sense of space below is tremendous. Indeed it might be argued that the Abbey is at its most numinous when it is empty altogether. In the semi-darkness it comes alive, authenticating its own inner life, testifying to Macaulay's description: 'This temple of silence and reconciliation where the enmities of a thousand years lie buried.'

Standing at the centre of the Crossing you are at the highest part of the building, some 157 feet, and if you then look along the North Transept – the Abbey is cruciform in its basic plan – you will notice a group of flags displayed over the door. These are the flags of the member states of the European Economic Community. I suspect that the Abbey is the only church which has them on permanent display. Their presence in a religious building suggests that concern for Europe has more to it than 'majoring' on the height of butter mountains. Indeed Europe embodies a culture derivative from Jerusalem, Athens, Rome, Christian Faith and modern science – not an inheritance to squander lightly.

Reaching St Edward's Chapel somewhat circuitously from the Crossing you confront the shrine and will be aware of a fifteenth-century screen which destroys the integrity of the basilica by dividing it into two and separating the royal tombs one from another. This surprising 'bifurcation' of one of the most satisfying and coherent areas in the Abbey is usually regarded as deliberately done in the mid-fifteenth century, though there is no manuscript evidence supporting this, to seal off an independent *cultus* around Henry v's Chantry Chapel which had begun to disturb the monks at their daily offices in the Choir. It seems the only possible *rationale* for an extraordinary act of near-vandalism.

Edward the Confessor's body rests in the Shrine behind the High Altar. Henry III in his reconstruction of the Norman Abbey east of the Choir Screen saw the Shrine of the Saint as central to his whole concept of a new Abbey. It was to pay Edward even more honour that the vast expenditure of money on a mammoth building programme was set in hand. It is difficult today to come to grips with a form of piety which expressed itself in this way. Reactions to the Shrine across the centuries have certainly varied from devotion or hostility to pure indifference. The monks of Westminster had a vested interest in keeping offertories at the

The Sovereign's stall in the choir when she attends services.

Shrine to a satisfactory level. Puritans and extreme Protestants generally, during and after the Reformation, regarded the Shrine as a superstitious relic of an unregenerate and papal past. In the eighteenth century Horace Walpole and his ilk treated such objects with a tolerant and yet superior ridicule. The Oxford Movement in going

Aymer de Valence, Earl of Pembroke, was victorious over King Robert of Scotland, and owned estates in England, Wales, Ireland and France. His tomb is a fine one and magnificently positioned in the Sanctuary.

The Chantry Chapel of Henry V (RIGHT), the folk hero of Agincourt, erected so that Masses might be said for the repose of his soul. 'If thou shouldst never see my face again, pray for my soul.'

back behind the Reformation to rediscover Anglican origins was more favourably inclined to such aids to devotion. Today ecumenicity and greater liturgical emphasis on the Eucharist have added to interest in the Shrine. Roman Catholic priests, on a significant saint's day, say their masses nearby and Anglican priests bring parochial parties to the Chapel. Perhaps a quickened interest in the somewhat eccentric Anglo-Saxon king indicates that people want to break out of the excessive conditioning of modern technology.

You leave the Shrine to move into Henry VII's Chapel. Here, in contrast to the Chapel of St Edward, you are conscious of entering another world, a world which in stretching out to the new has not yet forgotten the old. This Chapel retains something of the aura and mystique of a medieval past but at the same time witnesses to the articulation and rationality of the Renaissance.

Leaving the church by the East Cloister door, you are reminded immediately that the Collegiate Church of St Peter is living in the shell of a Benedictine monastery and that the history between monastery and Collegiate Church has been continuous. The monks lived and worked in the Cloisters, the officers in special cubicles; the monks' dormitory is now the Great Hall of Westminster School. The Library contains perhaps the finest collection of medieval monastic documents in Western Europe. The Norman Undercroft, part of Edward the Confessor's Abbey, now houses the Abbey museum and wax effigies. In the South Cloister is a door to the Song School through which the robed Choir processes into the Abbey along the West Cloister to sing Evensong.

This perfunctory glimpse at Westminster Abbey prompts the question: how did the Abbey of 1987 emerge from a little wooden church on Thorney Island to become the somewhat eccentric institution it is today.

*Dean's Yard (*RIGHT*) is the site of the old medieval barn. Now it is played in by choir-boys and scholars of Westminster School. 'We love the play-place of our early days' (William Cowper, 'Old Westminster').*

TWO

Origins

WESTMINSTER ABBEY was founded as a Benedictine Monastery by Edward, Saint, King and Confessor; and was consecrated on Holy Innocents' Day, 28 December 1065. This is solid, sober, historical fact. Not surprisingly, however, monkish chroniclers were not content to leave it at that and for a variety of reasons they pushed its origins back into a more remote past. It could well be that some of this legendary material has embedded within it a kernel of truth. Perhaps on the swamps of Thorney Island, where in primeval days the Giant Ox roamed freely, the Romans built a settlement and a Temple to Apollo, thus making it a sacred site. I like to think this is true, but interested as we may be, none of us can accept that an early Abbey was consecrated by St Peter, though this legend must have been a powerful weapon in the armoury of those monks seeking to prove that their Church was older than St Paul's. It could be, however, that in the days of St Dunstan (AD 909–88), there was a small community of monks on the island whom he protected from the ravages of the Danes. Certainly there was a wooden church there before Edward had finished his building operations.

With Edward the Confessor, in spite of his being a somewhat shadowy figure, we reach solid ground. Thorney Island, once a marshy wasteland, now rejoiced in 'fruitful fields and general cultivation'. A political assessment must be that Edward's inclination and talent fitted him more for the Cloister than the Throne. His reign was tempestuous, disturbed by conflicts between the Normans, with whom he surrounded himself, and the native English led by the formidable Earl Godwin. At his death, Edward left behind him a divided nation, having woefully neglected the welfare of his people.

Earlier in life Edward had solemnly promised to go on a pilgrimage to Rome and would have done so had he not been dissuaded by his Anglo-Saxon subjects, who feared the consequences of so long an absence. He was freed by the Pope from this

Edward the Confessor's Shrine.
His life was troubled and shot
through with conflicting loyalties.
'Sleep undisturbed, within this
peaceful Shrine, till angels wake
thee with a note like thine.'

enterprise on condition that he engaged in acts of charity to the poor and also that he built (or restored) a monastery at Westminster in honour of St Peter. This he did and the carrying out of this obligation became the major preoccupation of the later years of his reign. Building operations began in 1051, and the monastic domestic quarters were completed ten years later. Edward then turned to the church itself, in fact already begun, which he placed a little west of the old wooden construction so that the monks might carry on with their offering of the *opus dei* uninterrupted. It was still incomplete when consecrated on 28 December 1065.

On the very day of the consummation of his long-cherished hopes Edward was not present, being represented by his Queen, Edith. He was in fact lying prostrate in the Palace and when he was told that the consecration was over he rapidly grew worse, until on 3 January he lost the power of speech. Two days later he recovered this faculty and the Queen, so we are told, warmed his feet in her bosom. Archbishop Stigand and personal friends gathered round him and he rallied to prophesy that evil times would descend upon the land. His last thoughts were for his wife whom he commended to the Earl her brother; and the foreigners whom he had brought over with him that they might be cared for. Whether he commended the Earl as his successor no one can tell.

Edward, however, was not to be allowed to slip away into a forgotten past, remembered only as a somewhat inadequate ruler. He died on 5 January 1066 only to begin a posthumous existence which transcended and meant more than his earthly rule. He was buried, naturally, in his own church behind the High Altar.

History is full of paradoxes. None more so than that this eccentric monarch with an undoubted aura about him, last of the ancient royal house of Wessex, who had incurred severe criticism for surrounding himself with Normans, should now appear as the champion of a suppressed Englishry. Thus his so-called laws – they were not his – became a rallying point for a national sentiment. William the Conqueror, who claimed to be the legitimate successor of the Saxon King, thought it inexpedient to oppose this emerging cultus. The result was that finally, after much political chicanery and visits to Rome, Edward the Confessor was canonized by Pope Alexander III in 1161. The

celebration of this elevation must have been a great day at the Abbey, bringing to the monastery a unique prestige. It was, therefore, significant that at Henry III's coronation in 1220, the Confessor's sword was carried before the King, as part of the regalia, by the Earl of Chester.

The one date indelibly imprinted on the consciousness of the average Englishman is 1066. This is a sure instinct, for the Battle of Hastings was, and remains, a watershed in British history: its effects are still with us. The immediate outcome of this successful invasion and the death of Harold was the coronation of William on Christmas Day. This gave another sanction for his accession to the throne beyond the rights of conquest, a papal brief and the claim to legitimacy. It was a highly political act. History does not record, is indeed obstinately silent, as to how the Westminster monks reacted to what happened on that day. Almost certainly there must have been some in the community, including the ten whom Edward the Confessor brought from Exeter, whose origins were Anglo-Saxon and their sympathies with Harold, their lost leader.

It is difficult not to compare Edward the Confessor and William the Conqueror since both made their mark on the Abbey community in its early and formative years. Whereas the mystical, eccentric Edward sought in the Abbey a refuge from the cares and the chores of kingship, fencing himself in, William, the ruthless political operator, opened the doors of the Abbey to the realities of government and the exercise of power. Is it fanciful to suppose that here in this dichotomy between the two – Edward in spite of his faults and irresponsibilities setting his sights on God's Kingdom, William using the instruments of this world to bring tangible benefits to a divided nation – we find a tension, a duality, within which the Abbey has lived its life from the beginning? Every coronation bears testimony to this divide and seeks to bridge it. The beauty and transcendental quality of the Abbey's architectural structure may at times war with so much in the church that smacks of this world.

One of the fascinations of a Gothic building, so intricate and interlocking in design, is the unexpected view, the surprise, when by changing the perspective, new symmetries are discovered and a more transcendent and articulated beauty is apprehended. There is sense of peering into an unending recession with light at the end of the tunnel.

THREE

Two Churches

EDWARD THE CONFESSOR left behind him a superb and majestic church, a fine example of Norman architecture of the period at its best. Henry III did likewise some two centuries later, replacing Edward the Confessor's handiwork with a new building, equally fine, in the Gothic style.

Within and around these churches, a community, different in kind and in character, has lived its life for over nine hundred years. There have been periods of radical change, and an interregnum during the Commonwealth when it seemed that the inhabitants of the precincts had been dispersed, never to return. Still today the Abbey Church stands geographically where it has always stood, resplendent after restoration, greatly visited and admired. Still it gathers a 'family' around it, and visitors from all over the world.

The building, then, is central to this continuing life, and without it the community would not survive. But as the Church is necessary for the community so the community is necessary for the Church. Without the worship offered daily in the Abbey its heart would beat no more. A spiritual *rigor mortis* would set in. There is a monastic church in France much visited but in which no single act of worship takes place from year to year. The effect is as of an untimely death, a sense of desolation, a past betrayed. A church is more than an assemblage of stone and mortar: it is this and also what the worshipful community has made of it by prayer and devotion.

The concept of the Abbey was ambitious. Edward contributed lavishly from his own treasury to further it. To its progress he gave constant attention; and doubtless it was this, coupled with his being more or less on the spot, which kept the pace going, though the building was far from complete at the time of its consecration. Fortunately we know what its general appearance was. The famous Bayeux Tapestry was a political cartoon woven by the ladies of England or of Normandy. It provides a pathetic representation of the Confessor's funeral, depicting the cortège against the background of his new Abbey while the hand of God stretches out in blessing. The perspective of the whole strikes one as a little odd but from contemporary descriptions we may conclude that the Confessor's church had a long Nave and Transepts, a short Presbytery, very solid side walls and an eastern Apse. The ground plan was therefore cruciform and its total length was 332 feet, only a little less than Henry III's Abbey was to be. The curious used to be able to see, incised on the Nave floor, if they had good sight, the ground plan of Edward's building.

Knowledgeable people agree that in general the church at Westminster was similar to the Norman abbey at Jumièges, dedicated on 1 July 1067, now, alas, in ruins. This is not improbable, since Geoffrey of Jumièges was a friend and adviser to the Confessor from 1042 to 1052 and was in fact appointed by the Conqueror as Abbot of Westminster until removed for incompetence by him in 1075. Like many early Norman abbeys, Jumièges had two western towers, another over the Crossing; also a Nave of six double bays with alternate cruciform and square piers as at Westminster. William of Malmesbury writes of Edward's Abbey that it was the first great Romanesque church in England, 'which all now follow at great expense'.

In the general design of Edward the Confessor's Abbey his own hand can certainly be traced. He had spent many years in Normandy and thoroughly absorbed its spirit, so much so that the church which he built must have appeared almost alien in Anglo-Saxon England. Stephen Dykes Bower, a former Surveyor of the Fabric at the Abbey and a distinguished Gothicist, writes of it as 'an early manifestation of the paradox whereby the supremely national Church of England has been the least Anglican in its architectural manifestations'. This is in part due to its being a royal foundation responsive to the will of the monarch who had more than a national outreach. He also had access to money.

Some fragments of Edward's Norman Abbey at

least remain to point to past glories – two bays in the Chamber of the Pyx; fragments in the Undercroft; and a wall once part of the Refectory and now owned by Westminster School.

Edward, by universal assent, had built well and it might have been confidently expected that his Abbey, already hallowed by its association with the saintly King, would survive for future centuries. Why did this not prove to be the case? The answer is almost certainly twofold.

First, there had been a technological breakthrough in the science of building construction. One of the problems for the Norman builders was how to carry the weight and the thrust of the roof. Hence they tended to build 'low' and to install supporting columns of great girth. The flying buttress pressing in upon the external walls, quite apart from looking so fine, proved the answer to this difficulty. The result was that on the Continent, as in England, there was a spate of new buildings. Gothic architecture had arrived. Great cathedrals were being erected at Chartres, Évreux and Amiens and in England at Salisbury, Worcester and Lincoln. Set against the new magnificence, Edward's Abbey could well appear somewhat old-fashioned.

Second, Henry III's devotion to his saintly predecessor was real, not merely nominal. At his death in 1272 he chose to be buried in the tomb from which he himself had translated the body of the Confessor to its new Shrine, until his son Edward I prepared for him a more splendid tomb. Henry III, who regularly attended some three or four masses a day, felt that he could do better for the Confessor, pay him an even greater honour, if he were to build again and make his Shrine central to the new church. Henry III had a 'refined mind and cultivated tastes' and was intimately acquainted, through his marriage, with the arts and elegance of southern Europe. His own personal tastes were seen in the orders which he gave for the paintings to be executed at Westminster, Windsor, Woodstock and the Tower. The temptation to indulge his own tastes in the building of a new Abbey must have been strong, and he did not resist it. From his youth he had been familiar with building operations at the Abbey, and twenty years earlier he had laid the foundation stone for a new Lady Chapel planned by the monks. He was also at Ely in 1252 for the consecration of the Presbytery, which gave him an opportunity to see the work that English craftsmen were capable of performing.

He set about pulling down Edward's Abbey east of the Choir, and to build again, without counting the cost. (He was always incredibly extravagant.) Edward the Confessor was to be given a more splendid and jewel-bedecked shrine which took twenty years to construct. For twenty-six years, in spite of political crises and shortage of money, Henry III pushed on with his great enterprise, giving the various stages his personal oversight. Never perhaps had Henry undertaken a task which interested him more or gave him greater inner satisfaction. It ministered to many facets of his character, and it was often his own perfectionism which slowed down the pace of the building operations. Perhaps he was fortunate in that no societies for the protection of ancient buildings existed in those days, or the equivalent of the correspondence column in *The Times*.

By 1269 – he began operations in 1245 – the Apse, Presbytery and Crossing, plus the splendid Chapter House, were finished and in use. The great work was still proceeding when Henry died in 1272, leaving his own tomb unfinished. Even Edward I's coronation took place in a boarded-up and truncated church. The scene that greeted the new King must have been one of vivid contrasts as Henry's new church rose majestically over a huddle of closely packed buildings, new and old. To those well stricken in years it must have appeared unrecognizable.

The ambitious nature of the building programme may be seen from the following details. In charge of the day-to-day work was Edward, the Keeper of the Works – he certainly had the right Christian name – who held the office for twenty-five years and therefore probably made himself almost indispensable. In key positions were a master mason, a representative of the monastery, seven categories of workmen and a team of goldsmiths. The King himself was estimated to have spent some £50,000 on this vast project between the years 1245 and 1272. Even today when we have all learnt to add on the 'noughts', the following materials brought to the King's Quay are impressive: hundreds of boatloads of ragstone from Kent and Caen, sometimes as many as two hundred in five weeks; tin from Cornwall; Purbeck marble from Dorset; lead from Derbyshire; and structural timber from the King's forests in Essex and Kent. In one week during 1253 a total of 391 workmen,

Edward the Confessor's Abbey which took some fifty years to build must have been a veritable hive of activity. Casualties were high in the course of its construction.

Edward the Confessor's Shrine. The sick were brought here for healing.

carpenters, marblers, smiths, painters and glaziers were at work on the building. There were also the casual labourers such as William the swineherd, who was paid 21s 7d for digging and carrying a thousand cart-loads of sand between April and December in 1253. It was a vast cooperative enterprise.

The master mason in charge of the overall plan and its execution was Henry de Reyns to whom Henry III gave the briefing that as well as honouring Edward the Confessor's Shrine as a focal point for the whole design it was necessary to make special provision for a coronation church; and this meant leaving a space near the High Altar and Crossing on which coronations could be staged. This was faithfully carried out. It was by the King's deliberate choice that his new Abbey showed evident signs of Norman influence. Thus in certain respects Westminster Abbey as a whole remains unique though elements in it have been copied. The parish church of Stone in Kent (well worth a visit) has affinities with the Abbey which have led some to suggest that the same designer was responsible for both. Yet in emphasizing a Norman influence it would be wrong to exclude English execution and English skill, so much so that if Henry's Abbey could be whisked away and planted in Normandy it would be felt to be different from other abbeys around. It may be that, contrary to the usual view, this was due to the fact that Henry did not choose a French designer but an English one whom he sent abroad to absorb the new Gothic in such a place as Reims, then leaving him free to do as he felt proper. If this is true it may account for the restraint of the Abbey as compared with the extravagances of the cathedrals at Cologne, Beauvais and Amiens. Dykes Bower writes: 'The proportions of the Abbey are so perfectly adjusted, its actual design and relationship of parts so good, that the interior is completely satisfying.'

The new Shrine was central to Henry's whole concept and here he imported craftsmen and material from Italy to measure up to his own perfectionism. He gave it added glory by placing the golden Shrine on a marble and mosaic base, decorating it with small statuettes of saints and kings. Over it was a canopy which could be raised and lowered at will. It needs to be remembered that until the fifteenth century there was no screen behind the High Altar, thus making the Shrine easily visible from the West End of the Abbey.

Thus was built one of the three great shrines of medieval England, to match those of St Thomas of Canterbury and our Lady of Walsingham. Of these only the Shrine of St Edward survives, and it is sadly mutilated. That it has survived at all is probably due to Henry VIII who was reluctant for a king to be dishonoured at a time when he was concerned to give prestige to the new Tudor monarchy. The Shrine was removed from the Chapel during the reign of Edward VI when the Continental Reformation was at its most extreme in England, but was put back during the Roman Catholic revival under Queen Mary. Those who then restored the Shrine certainly botched the job since it is off-centre, columns are missing (one is upside down) and its gold embellishments have disappeared. It is a caricature of what it once was, an offence to the artist who conceived it and to the craftsmen who skilfully worked upon it. It is difficult now to see it within the context of giving glory to God.

There are those who hold that the spoliation of the Shrine is a part of English history and witnesses to extreme Protestant feeling in the middle years of the sixteenth century. To restore it would

be to destroy and falsify a piece of significant English past.

The other view asserts, equally strongly, that to continue to perpetuate a 'botched' job which is a complete and unlovely travesty of what the designer intended is totally unfair and really quite reprehensible. (As the result of intensive research over many years an architect, Mr O'Neilly, has been able to recover its original design and has embodied this in a model.) History is important, but surely the claim might equally be made that part of this self-same history was the laying up in the fourteenth century of a magnificent work of art in St Edward's Shrine. I have to confess I veer to the latter of these two views.

Another example of a more extreme kind is the wooden effigy of Henry v which, recumbent, lies under his Chantry Chapel and was originally encased in silver, the head being of solid silver. Within a few years all the silver was stripped off by robbers, leaving a headless trunk. The effigy has now been given back a fine head in polyester resin, and when this was done an effort was made to secure as accurate a representation of Henry as possible. Was *this* the violation of a history which ought to be preserved? In this particular case the

Masons carrying out repair work, a never-ending task. Theirs is a high skill, fortunately now reviving.

Abbey authorities were in fact criticized because it was impossible, so critics asserted, to be sure that the new head was an exact replica of the original. No one in his senses, of course, wishes to run round the Abbey to encourage 'conjectural restorations'; but, as Aristotle has taught us, there is a mean between two extremes.

No building, not least a church, can remain static year in year out, because it houses a living community; also emergent needs for worship can affect its structure. The Abbey as it is today is certainly not the Abbey as Henry III left it. Succeeding generations have tried to enrich it. A spectacular adornment to the Abbey was the Cosmati floor given by Abbot Ware in 1268, named after the famous Cosmati family which worked with mosaics in Rome during the thirteenth century. Throughout the Sanctuary and St Edward's Chapel 'the most highly wrought Cosmati pavement ever erected' was installed. Cosmati work consists of coloured pieces of stone arranged in intriguing and intricate patterns. The tragedy is that this example of quite superb craftsmanship has now permanently to be kept under a carpet because of the disastrous use of a soft English Purbeck for the interlacing bands instead of a harder marble from the Continent.

A further innovation in the Abbey which led to an unexpected result was the establishment of Henry v's Chantry Chapel east of the Shrine. The victor of Agincourt was on the way to becoming a folk hero at the time of his death, and masses for the repose of his soul were said daily in his Chapel. The installation, in such a strategic position, of almost a rival cultus must have been most disturbing to the monks as they performed their *opus dei* in the Choir. Their response, in the mid-fifteenth century, was to erect a tall screen immediately behind the High Altar which effectively cuts off St Edward's Chapel, thus immunizing it effectively from what was happening down below in the Choir. (The explanation suggested here for what the monks did – Abbot Harwden probably inspired it – has no manuscript evidence to support it but is, for the moment, the most cogent.)

It was an odd thing to do. It ruins the integrity of the Apse and separates the royal tombs by a great divide. This could never have been perpetrated so long as devotion to St Edward ran high. Henry III had surely intended that the Shrine, deliberately placed at a different level in relation to the Cross-

Henry III's fine tomb, prepared by his son Edward I, befits the second founder of Westminster Abbey. His heart he bequeathed to the Abbess of Fontevrault.

Henry VII spared no expense and ransacked Europe to beautify and give distinction to his Chapel. It contains an embarrassment of riches. The statuettes, which are many, are perfectly executed. One wears spectacles and one lady sports a beard!

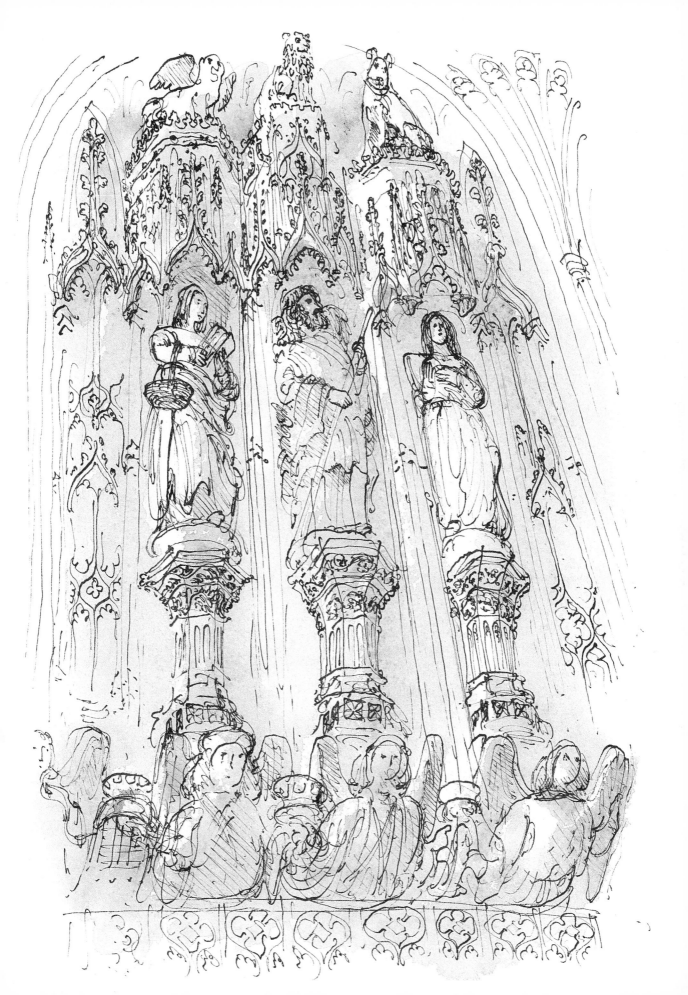

ing and Choir, should be visible from the west end of the Nave. On the screen there are depicted incidents in the life of Edward the saintly King. Perhaps this *amende honorable* served to mollify a number of uneasy consciences. I cannot believe that this step was taken *nemine contradicente,* but must have been a talking point at the time.

The most significant and memorable addition to the Abbey, indeed one of its chief glories, is the Chapel of King Henry VII, a monarch who in some ways bears comparison with William the Conqueror. Both took over a divided nation as the result of a military victory; both had to stabilize their thrones and to establish law and order after years of near anarchy; both were ruthless political operators. Frugal and parsimonious, Henry was determined as a comparative *parvenu* to enhance the status of the Tudor monarchy and to do this by spending lavishly on building one of the most beautiful of all chapels as a burial place for Henry VI. (In fact after three churches had laid claim to his body, Westminster, Chertsey and Windsor, it was finally the last of these which proved successful.) Stowe writes in his chronicle: 'This year the

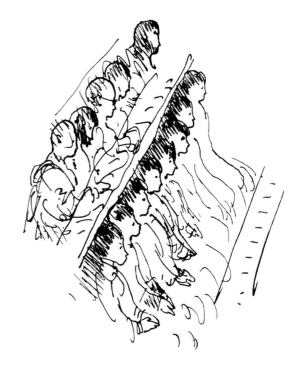

Chappell of our Ladie above the east end of the high altar of Westminster Church with also a taverne neere adjoyning called the White Rose, were taken downe; in the which place or plot of ground, on 24 January, 1502/3 the first stone of our Lady Chappell was laid by the hands of John Islip, abbot of the same monastery.'

Ten years later the whole structure was complete, except, of course, for the effigies of Henry VII and his Queen commissioned from the Italian craftsman Torrigiani (who also made the recumbent bronze figure of Henry's mother, Margaret Beaufort – see p101). It was Henry's wish that their bodies should be interred in a black and white tomb in the centre of the Chapel. In fact this royal desire was not implemented, for the tomb was placed at the east end of the Chapel, surrounded by a quite remarkable grille. It was estimated that some £14,000 was spent on the Chapel, a vast sum for those days, and, as we have suggested, Henry did not spare himself. To quote his own words: '... as for the price and value ... our mind is that they be such as apperteyneth to a Prince'. The result was a building which has been fittingly described as 'grand and sumptious ... pre-eminently English'. It was not only a matter of money: Henry ransacked Europe for craftsmen and artists. He was fortunate in his two architects,

probably the brothers Robert and William Vertue, who along with genius displayed genuine humility. They were careful not to vie with the structure and proportions of the Abbey, to which they showed a well-merited deference. Thus the east end of the Apse was not unlike the one it displaced; the height does not compete with either the Choir or Transepts; nor does it deny light to the Abbey. The brothers Vertue were also themselves fortunate in the architectural climate of their day. The Middle Ages, with their mystique and faith, were not sunk without trace; yet the rationality and articulation of the Renaissance were already a potent force. The Vertue brothers were not indifferent to either. Old and new are blended in a satisfying resolution, and the fan-vaulted roof never ceases to please. The disappearance of certain windows has deprived the Chapel of colour, but the banners of members of the Order of the Bath have reintroduced it.

Amongst the many distinguished architects who have served the Abbey perhaps the best known as a national figure was Sir Christopher Wren, though his work at the Abbey does not bear comparison with what he did for St Paul's after its destruction in the Great Fire. Sir Christopher's main concern while at the Abbey was the need for a systematic repair of stonework. However, certain 'lacunae' in the structure of the building, he believed, should also be attended to. In order to promote this, he drew up a paper for the benefit of the Dean and Chapter calling attention to three desiderata necessary for 'a proper completing of what is left imperfect'. They were: (1) the erection of a 'lofty spire' as originally intended, which 'will give a proper grace to the whole fabric and [to] the west end of the city which seems to want it'; (2) the finishing of the two Western Towers; and (3) the making of the North Front more magnificent. Of these three, one still remains to be accomplished.

It is reasonable to suppose, as did Sir Christopher, that the original intention was to build a central spire. Whether this did not happen because it was felt that the building could not carry the weight or because there was no money available we cannot tell. Sir Christopher constructed a model, complete with a spire, now on display in the North Transept. Other contemporary paintings of the Abbey also show a spire already *in situ*. This lack is an impoverishment, particularly in view of the tall buildings along Victoria Street, which now com-

pete, in height successfully, with the Abbey.

The second desideratum, the completion of the two Western Towers, has been achieved, not directly by Sir Christopher Wren it is true, but through his successor as surveyor, Nicholas Hawksmoor, who at the age of eighteen became Wren's 'scholar and domestic clerk'. His output of work, original and for purposes of restoration, was remarkable. He did not share the strong contemporary aversion to Gothic, possibly through his having learnt to admire it at Beverley Minster, the only building in England which in any respect, at that time, resembled the Abbey. Dykes Bower writes:

What is significant is that so classical an architect as Hawksmoor never doubted that the towers must be Gothic, and that he knew how to make them so. Nowhere else did he succeed so well when using a tongue of whose grammar he was not master. These towers in some curious way – but really because of their latent historical strength – seem so natural a part of the Abbey fabric that they have become almost its symbol of identification. It is this aspect which identifies the Abbey to the world.

The third desideratum, 'the making of the North Front more magnificent', has certainly been achieved, though some have been critical, I think unfairly, of the result. Gilbert Scott, Surveyor in the mid-nineteenth century, entirely redesigned the entry into the Abbey by the North Door. Until the recent cleaning it was concealed under dirt, decay, and grime, so much so that a former Abbey surveyor remarked that once the Abbey was cleaned people would rediscover the genius of Scott. This is precisely what has happened, and the result is spectacular. The Front is seen as it has not been for centuries. Small statues can be detected hitherto concealed, and the flying buttresses are shown to good effect.

The Abbey has never been in a position to be financially independent. It was the contention of the Dean and Chapter that when Queen Elizabeth entrusted the Abbey to them in 1560 the building was in a decayed condition, but though they had been given resources sufficient to pay annual bills and maintenance no resources had been allocated adequate to undertake capital expenditure on the building. Sir Christopher Wren maintained that there had been centuries of neglect on the stonework and roof, which had led to the then critical condition, coupled with certain defects in the original design – 'the pride of a very high roof raised above reasonable pitch is not for duration, for the lead is apt to slip'. Also the choice of Reigate stone was a mistaken one since it absorbed water and thus suffered from frost. A schedule of needed restoration was drawn up and Parliament donated a tax on seacoal to make this possible. It was only by large grants from the Board of Works that extensive repairs on Henry VII's Chapel were undertaken at the beginning of the nineteenth century.

In other words, over a long period after the establishment of the Collegiate Church of St Peter in Westminster all major repairs on the Abbey were effected through state aid. Although the need for continual repair work on the Abbey remained, this source of supply dried up and governments have felt themselves unable to give direct subventions to the Dean and Chapter in this way. Thus the Abbey was forced to organize its own appeals for general restoration work. This did not apply

only to stonework but also to the Henry VII's Chapel roof which early in its life through some mistake by those who originally placed it in position, needed attention, as did the gigantic roof over the Nave. Faced with these and other commitments, Dean Ryle's Appeal was launched in 1920, and then the Coronation Appeal in 1953 for a million pounds from a million people. The latter exceeded its target, but only because of a number of large donations.

The fan vaulted ceiling of Henry VII Chapel is a great glory.

The mason's craft is as old as civilization itself to which its skills have liberally contributed. The Abbey is helping to revive it through the great work of restoration now going on.

The sight of the Western towers means for people the world over only one thing – Westminster Abbey.

Still the insatiable thirst of the Dean and Chapter for money, essential for the maintenance of the building, persisted. Hence the Westminster Abbey Trust was set up in 1972, the Dean and Chapter having the good fortune to secure as president of the Trust the Duke of Edinburgh, and a group of distinguished donor trustees. So far the Trust has raised, without any public appeal, no less than eight million pounds. It needs, probably, another four million, but already the result has been such that the Abbey can now be seen, externally, in its pristine condition, as it has not been seen for centuries. This restoration represents the most extensive work on the church since Henry III built it. At the moment, the Western Towers, still uncleaned, stick out like a sore thumb. Work is to commence soon and the scaffolding is already up.

FOUR

'In Quires and Places where they Sing'

WESTMINSTER ABBEY was conceived as an 'act of worship in stone' and therefore uniquely fitted to house a group of religious whose primary function was to offer their whole lives, corporately and individually, to praise God and witness to his perfect kingdom. Central to this offering, informing all that they did, whether in Cloister, Chapter House or Church, was their coming together to sing the divine office in the Choir. Thus it was supremely in the performance of these daily acts of worship that study and physical labour, which filled the rest of the day, found and sustained their inspiration. In a world of flux and change they sought '*stabilitas*', permanence, symbolized in their being tied to one place of residence. So did the rhythm of their Offices, interspersed over day and night, measure up to the boast of the Psalmist: 'Seven times a day do I praise thee.' In a fallen world they set out, *dei gratia*, to be a light shining in dark places.

Throughout the five hundred years of the monastery's existence at Westminster the *opus dei*, which included such services as Prime, Terce, Sext, Nones, Compline, were sung to plainsong.

Is there such a thing as religious music, religious not only in that it is used within a worshipful context? If so, is plainsong unique in coming into this category? And what is there about certain kinds of music which make them religious? Most people would conceive of such music, if it exists, as capable of evoking emotions and attitudes felt to be religious, such as love, penitence, awe and adoration. Plato would have had no hesitation whatever in answering 'Yes' to the question, and that is why in his *Republic* he applies a strict censorship, banning certain harmonies as inimical to virtue. Chairman Mao Tse-tung, and at times the Russian Government, have taken the same view, hence the condemnation of 'bourgeois' music. Certainly Purcell's settings for morning and evening prayer differ in their character according to whether they were to be sung at Whitehall or in Westminster Abbey. Maybe he would have accounted for this distinction in terms of the musical resources available.

There are those who would argue that plainsong, in the restraint of its melodic line, in its emphasis on the community rather than on the individual and its refusal to 'show off', brings with it an authentic religious emotion. It avoids the unhealthy introversion and self-pity generated by over-sentimentalized melodies and somewhat sugary harmonies. Many composers, however, would claim that there are only two kinds of music – good and bad.

The level of spirituality at Westminster waxed and waned. The Customary of 1266 suggests a high level of devotion achieved by certain members of the community. Some of the brethren, we are told, 'when they hear the bell are accustomed to listen intently to God's messenger saying to them: "Behold the Bridegroom comes, go out to meet him." At midnight, the hour of Christ's birth, a few monks privately repeated to themselves: "Blessed be that hour when Christ was born of the Virgin Mary." '

The choir offices, as well as the private devotions of individual monks, did not exhaust the worshipful life of the community. The ecclesiastical calendar included many Saints' Days (observed by a Mass with solenmnity and high ceremonial), not least those associated with their founder, St Edward, King and Confessor. In addition there were anniversaries connected with Queen Eleanor (wife of Edward I), Richard II, and Henry V, to mention but a few. Some chapels, such as that of Our Lady of the Pew, had their own cultus. Particular high spots, in being domestic and leading to reunions, were two preaching days, Palm Sunday and Good Friday, when young Westminster monks who were carrying on with their studies at Gloucester College, Oxford, were brought to the Abbey and delivered sermons. These were expected to address the brethren with greater theological insight than the average monk could command. Coronations – in all nineteen were held during the community's existence – must have made excitement run high. The ceremony itself was framed within the Eucharist and sometimes there were political complications, which must have had repercussions on the community as well as on the monarch.

With the coming of the Reformation in the sixteenth century and the consequent break with Rome the liturgical pattern of the *Ecclesia Anglicana* and therefore of Westminster Abbey was radically changed. The Book of Common Prayer replaced the missals and the breviaries of the Roman Catholic Church: plainsong as a staple diet went out, Anglican chants came in. It is easy to exaggerate and to forget that much of worth was piloted over from the old to the new. The Charter given to Westminster Abbey in 1560, together with the Statutes which Elizabeth omitted to sign, made it clear that the worship of Almighty God was still a prime responsibility; and that this should be offered by a Choral Foundation singing the reformed daily offices in the same Choir Stalls as were formerly occupied by the monks.

For the emerging Church of England it was imperative that a new liturgy should be devised, preserving what was valuable in the old but open to the best of the new contemporary Protestantism. Thomas Cranmer, a University don whose interest throughout life was the study of liturgy, was chosen to perform this task. There were three key principles which he sought to embody in reshaping the liturgy of the Church of England: (1) that it be in the vernacular – 'understanded of the people'; (2) that it be designed for use by ordinary men and women in the parishes up and down the country; and (3) that it be theologically inclusive, not provocative but eirenical – that is, the mean between two extremes.

To secure this, Cranmer used the old choir offices, for example in the *Sarum rite*, telescoping them into the two services of Morning and Evening Prayer. He also took over and redrafted the services of baptism and marriage, the Lord's Supper or Holy Communion, and incorporated them into the Edward VI Prayer Books of 1549 and 1552. There were further small changes in Elizabeth's reign until fixity was reached, upon the Restoration of Charles II, in the definitive 1662 edition of the Book of Common Prayer.

An attempt was made in 1689 to revise this Prayer Book as the result of the setting up by King

Stalls in Henry VII Chapel, many having their individual misericords imaginatively conceived.

Chapel of St Nicholas, patron saint of children (LEFT). Attendance at Mass here, carried with it the additional benefit of an indulgence for three years and sixty days, doubtless a very nice and subtle mathematical calculation.

The monks at Westminster kept up a rhythm of prayer throughout the twenty-four hours. Here we see them 'untimely ripp'd' from their beds, entering the Abbey for the Night Office. 'Seven times a day do I praise Thee.'

William III of a commission which met, as Thomas Sprat's guests, in Jerusalem Chamber – then, as now, part of the Deanery at Westminster Abbey. The intention was to make a last effort to bring Dissenters back into the Church of England and to do this by revising the Prayer Book more to their liking. The result was a revision which was liberal and rationalistic in character. However, this brave attempt was singularly unsuccessful. Not all members of the commission turned up at its first session. Thomas Sprat, Dean of Westminster, who was obviously embarrassed by his royal nomination to this body, immediately questioned the legality of their proceedings, and finally withdrew. So intense was the opposition to this attempt at Prayer Book revision that it was never put before Convocation and existed only in manuscript until published in the nineteenth century. Cranmer's work, with its dignified, felicitous and economical use of language, survived until well on in the twentieth century.

The ending of the near monopoly of plainsong, which Reformers regarded as a relic of Popish superstition, providentially came at a time when talented composers such as Thomas Tallis, William Byrd (he remained a life-long Roman Catholic), Thomas Weelkes, and the brothers Tomkins were busily engaged in making music for the Church. The new vernacular Prayer Book gave them full scope, since chants for the Psalms, settings for the Canticles and scores for Anthems were needed for use in 'Quires and Places where they sing'. Westminster Abbey was conspicuously one of these. That so many outstanding composers of the day should elect to write music for the new liturgy, as well as delight their contemporaries with songs and madrigals, was a good augury for the future. It is a tradition which has been continued over the centuries until today and to which eloquent testimony is paid in the Musicians' Aisle in Westminster Abbey.

The organists and Masters of the Choristers from the sixteenth to the twentieth century who served the Abbey make an impressive list. Many of their compositions are part of the heritage of English church music and are sung far beyond Britain, indeed throughout the world-wide Anglican Communion. If one does make a choice from the earlier composers, that is between Byrd, Orlando and Christopher Gibbons, John Blow, William Croft and Henry Purcell, pride of place

should probably be given to the last on this list.

Purcell was in every respect a native of Westminster, born and bred in the city, and a chorister at the Chapel Royal. This led almost inevitably to a distinguished musical career at the Abbey, at Court and in the theatre. His virtuosity was such that he became equally at home in writing the kind of music appropriate and acceptable in all these institutions. He died on 21 November 1695 and the esteem of his contemporaries was clearly indicated at his funeral. The Dean and Chapter were present in full force, dressed in their copes, while the choirs of the Abbey and the Chapel Royal sang the 'dirges' which Purcell had composed for the funeral of 'her late Majesty [Queen Mary] of ever blessed memory'. A person present writes of Purcell as 'one of the most celebrated Masters of the Science of Music in the Kingdom and scarce inferior to any in Europe'.

Amongst the most colourful of Abbey organists, son of a more famous father, Orlando, was Christopher Gibbons (1615–76), who gained a reputation as a dashing Cavalier during the Civil War, for which he was rewarded at the Restoration by becoming apprentice organist of both Westminster Abbey and the Chapel Royal. He successfully built up the musical foundation after its dispersal for the sixteen years of the Commonwealth. He was forced to begin with men only until the boys could be properly trained. Christopher Gibbons was also organist at the time of Charles II's Coronation, a splendid affair. Anthony à Wood, of whom it was said that he 'never spake well of any man', dismisses Christopher Gibbons, probably unfairly, as a 'grand debauchee' and asserts that he would 'often sleep at Morning Prayers when he was to play the organ'.

Certainly the organ loft over the centuries became at times a focal point for tension and disturbance, particularly when the organist tended to hold a private court there. Something like this seems to have happened with Christopher Gibbons, since the Dean and Chapter on 18 December 1660 passed the following resolution: 'It was ordered that the Backe door of the Organ Loft should be shutt upp ... and that neither the Organist nor any other permitt any person to bee in the Organ Loft during the time of divine service and that the Organist and the blower keep themselves private and not expose themselves to the view of the people during their stay in the Organ

Loft.' There are stories of a lady tracking an organist down after having travelled thousands of miles and thrusting her unwelcome presence upon him in the organ loft.

When I first went to the Abbey stories concerning Sir Frederick Bridge, the organist, were still current around the Precincts. At a reception in College Garden I recall an ex-chorister of ninety reminiscing about his first appearance at a sung Evensong, doubtless a most traumatic experience. When it came to the versicles and responses, a senior boy next to him sang: 'God shave the Queen'. All his nervousness and pent-up emotions suddenly dissolved into a burst of loud laughter. Immediately after the service he received a peremptory summons to see Sir Frederick in the organ loft. The latter was not pleased and had some very tough things to say to the erring chorister. His fierce lecture over, his mood sud-

The daughter of Edward Talbot, Vth Earl of Shrewsbury, depicted on his tomb in St Edmund's Chapel.

denly changed as he put his hand in his cassock pocket and gave him a sweet, dismissing him with the words: 'Run away and *never* do this again!' He assured me he never did.

Sir Frederick Bridge brought the choir school up to date and let it be known that there would be full rehearsals and that all would be required to turn up to them. The organ was rebuilt under his guidance and Pearson's fine case put into position. He was responsible for the music at the coronations of Edward VII and George V.

During the long course of its history as a Collegiate Church there have only been two periods when the Choral Foundation was dispersed. The first was the years of the Commonwealth in the seventeenth century, when the Anglican Liturgy with its sung services ceased; the organs were not simply removed but broken up; and the choir was disbanded. John Vicars, 'schoolmaster, poetaster and polemic', who, we are assured, could 'out-scold the boldest face at Billingsgate', expressed his virulent Puritan convictions when he wrote with great satisfaction of Westminster Abbey during these years:

> . . . a most rare and strange alteration of the face of things in the Cathedral [*sic*] Church of Westminster. Namely that whereas there was wont to be heard nothing almost but roaring-Boys and squeaking organ-pipes, and the Cathedrall Catches of Morley and I know not what trash; now the popish altar is quite taken away, the bellowing organs are demolish't and pulled down and the treble or trouble and base singers, chanters or inchanters driven out and instead thereof, there is now set up a most blessed Orthodox Preaching Ministry . . . Our God what a rich and rare alteration! What a strange change indeed!

Not everyone, of course, would agree with Vicars in seeing this change as for the better. One can but speculate as to whether the singers and clergy extruded during the Commonwealth wondered if they would ever return to their old familiar haunts.

The second occasion when the Choral Foundation was for the time being disbanded was during the Second World War. On its outbreak – H.G.Wells had prepared everyone for instant annihilation – the boys were immediately evacuated to Christ's Hospital near Horsham in Sussex, where they remained till 1941, being rehearsed regularly. The Dean and Chapter then decided, reluctantly, to dispense with the choris-

Looking towards 'College', the house of the Queens' scholars of Westminster School, pioneered by Sir Christopher Wren and completed by Nicholas Hawksmoor. In the College Garden during the Middle Ages were the herb garden and the oyster beds.

ters, arranging where possible for them to continue their education in cathedral schools located in places of relative safety. Meanwhile daily services were sung in the Abbey by lay vicars, who were joined in due course by boys recruited locally by the faithful sub-organist, Dr Osborne Peasgood. To begin with this choir sang only on Sundays but soon there were added high days and certain weekdays. This group continued to sing until the choir school was reopened in 1947, the first service entirely sung by the restored choir being on Friday, 6 June 1947. The music on this historic occasion consisted of the Canticles sung to plainsong with faux-bourdon by Tallis and the anthem, most appropriately, 'O Lord increase our Faith' by Orlando Gibbons. It was some time before the choir, under Dr William McKie, was back to normal – or perhaps on to a different normality. Traditions, once broken, are not easily restored.

Because of those traditions, its endowed Choral Foundation, and the sheer size of the building, the Abbey has played an important part in the history and development of English music. It has not only responded to ecclesiastical and liturgical needs, but has set the lead in the production of large musical works deploying a considerable choir and orchestra. In this the Abbey celebration of the Handel Centenary in 1784 established a precedent that others have not been slow to follow. This remarkable event, directed by Joah Bates, attracted the patronage of George III. On 26 May a miscellaneous programme was put on at the Abbey and three days later a performance of *The Messiah*. On the express command of the King, the Abbey performances were repeated on 3 and 5 June. The preparation for them was elaborate and constituted a veritable transformation in the general appearance of the Abbey. A stage for the chorus and orchestra reaching to the level of the great West Window was put at the end of the Nave, on which was placed the organ with a detached keyboard. From here Joah Bates 'directed his forces'. Seating was provided for 3,000 people on the floor of the Nave. The King himself was 'high and lifted up' in a royal box west of the choir

screen, facing the audience. Indeed, he and his family attended all the celebrations. The number of musicians involved merits the much overdone adjective 'fantastic'. In particular the choir consisted of 60 trebles (mostly boys), 48 counter tenors, 83 tenors and 84 bass. The orchestra numbered about 250. Nothing on this scale had ever been attempted in England before. Some critics were doubtful whether so many participants located in such a building as the Abbey could hope to play in tune or in time, and whether the noise would be bearable. Such fears were groundless. So successful was this venture that three more festivals were held in successive years. The last of these was the most ambitious of all. It was on this occasion that the King, overcome with emotion, rose to his feet during the Hallelujah Chorus to be joined by the whole audience. Joseph Haydn, seated near His Majesty, wept.

Sir William McKie writes that these musical occasions in the Abbey were of major importance in establishing an English tradition of large amateur choirs singing Handel. One wonders how far Handel himself would have approved.

George Frederick Handel, composer of the immortal oratorio The Messiah. *'I did think I did see all Heaven before me and the great God himself.'*

GEORGE FREDERICK HANDEL

John of Eltham, Earl of Cornwall, second son of Edward II lived his life dangerously. He died at Perth when only nineteen years of age. He was three times regent of England, and quelled numerous Scottish border raids. At a midnight funeral in 1776 the beautiful canopy on his tomb was demolished when a mass of masonry collapsed. Such funerals were in future firmly prohibited. 'One crowded hour of glorious life, is worth an age without a name.'

In 1874 Sir Joseph Barnby directed at the Abbey one of the first performances in England, certainly the first in an English church, of Bach's *St Matthew* Passion, a precedent to be revived years later by the Westminster Abbey Special Choir. On Thursday, 6 December 1962, there was heard in the Abbey the second performance of Benjamin Britten's *War Requiem* – the first was in Berlin – conducted by Britten himself. At the reception afterwards I had the temerity to ask him whether he thought he had laid up a work for posterity. He replied courteously to this somewhat naive question that his main concern was to address a contemporary generation on the evils and tragedy of war. He has certainly done this.

Another Requiem of a different genre had its second performance in the Abbey – the first in this case was in New York – namely Andrew Lloyd Webber's *Requiem*, written originally in memory of his father, a distinguished musician. I can't but recall that as a very young boy, way back in 1953, when an appeal was launched to 'Save Westminster Abbey from decay and ruin', he emptied his money box and sent the contents to the Abbey to prevent this seemingly imminent calamity. It contained about eight shillings. When he was given to understand that this had proved inadequate to complete the work of restoration he emptied it a second time and sent in a further donation.

It has been the custom for the Abbey to mark by an act of worship certain occasions significant in its own history. This goes back to the days of the Middle Ages. Such was the case on 3 June 1760, when the Collegiate Church celebrated the two hundredth anniversary of the Charter granted to it by Queen Elizabeth I. This was entirely a domestic affair. The Dean, Dr Zachary Pearce, preached a sermon, concluding with these worthy if rather self-evident words: 'Let us all remember constantly and faithfully, to put into practice everything which our several duties require; with grateful hearts for the benefits which we enjoy and a strong desire to make those benefits our own by our behaviour.'

Zachary Pearce may be taken as a typical eighteenth-century Dean (1756–68) in contrast to the handsome dynamic and Jacobite Francis Atterbury. Pearce was a classical scholar remembered only by an élitist few as the editor of Longinus, a

Greek rhetorician. In common with most ecclesiastics of his age he deplored the excesses of 'enthusiasm'; was kindly and the first Dean of Westminster to resign the Bishopric of Rochester but only after great difficulty. In old age he longed for release from his labours and anticipated this in somewhat innocuous verse:

> From all decanal cares at last set free
> (I would that freedom still more perfect be)
> My Sun's meridian, How long past and gone
> And Night, unfit for work, now hastening on,
> In Life's late Evening, thro' a light of day
> I find me gently tending to decay!

One cannot see him being considered for mem-

Sir Humphrey Bourgchier, killed fighting for Edward IV at the Battle of Barnet.

orialization in Poets' Corner nor joining Wesley to engage in open-air preaching. For him the liturgy of 1662 had to be preserved inviolate and without change.

A radically new approach to the conduct of worship, including the Communion, was brought to the Abbey by Dr Jocelyn Perkins, who joined the staff as a minor canon on the very day that the bells were ringing at the Abbey for the relief of Mafeking in 1900, and later became Sacrist. When he took up his responsibilities he soon decided that the ordering of services was slipshod and that he must progressively take this matter in hand. In arriving at this decision Dr Perkins had certain advantages. He knew exactly what he wanted.

During his sixty years at the Abbey he had watched deans and canons come and go, confi-

dent that time was on his side and therefore that he could achieve his objectives piecemeal. He suffered from deafness, which made it possible for him never to hear an order from the Dean unless he happened to approve of it.

Perkins recognized the need to use the space in the Abbey by introducing movement and colour into the ceremonial. Hence the acquisitions of vestments – copes – to be worn in the many processions. His desire was to make the Abbey way of doing things a pattern while seeing its facilities as *sui generis* even to the extent of having its own colour sequence which, he maintained – rightly or wrongly – went back to medieval times. As Sacrist he had a particular responsibility for the Sacristy which he increasingly furnished. He gathered around him an enthusiastic group of Old Choris-

ters and from these established the Brotherhood of St Edward which assisted at the Sung Eucharist and at many a special service. He rehearsed them thoroughly and won their respect, even affection. Rehearsals had their occasional excitements, even embarrassments. On one such occasion in relation to the Battle of Britain Service his watchful eye concentrated on two greatly bemedalled officers who were carrying the RAF flag through the Nave to the High Altar. This having been successfully negotiated a very stern voice echoed down the Abbey: 'Do it again and this time do it in step!'

So Dr Perkins established a new approach to worship and, though academic liturgiologists were sometimes critical of its lack of theological insight, he transformed the presentation, giving it movement, colour and dramatic effect. He took full advantage of the building and many a parish priest would visit the Abbey seeking inspiration.

I was responsible for securing the publication of his *Sixty Years at Westminster Abbey*. (He wrote

William of Colchester (d.1420), one of the great medieval abbots, followed the equally distinguished Nicolas Litlyngton. He carried on with the great work of rebuilding the Nave, assisted liberally by grants from Richard II and Henry V. He was accused of involvement in a plot to restore Richard being sent for a short period to the Tower.

In the North Cloister (RIGHT), where the office holders had their cubicles, the monks did their serious work.

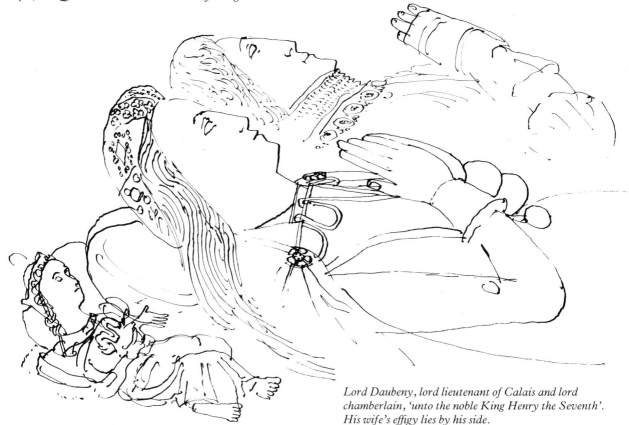

Lord Daubeny, lord lieutenant of Calais and lord chamberlain, 'unto the noble King Henry the Seventh'. His wife's effigy lies by his side.

extensively, not least for the Alcuin Press.) A number of pages in the manuscript were missing and I had the task of filling in the gaps, using, of course, the colourful prose of which he was a master. This I did with such success that I cannot myself now detect which pages are mine! As a frontispiece I used a brilliant cartoon of him by Christopher Hildyard, his successor as Sacrist. However, I was uneasy as to what Dr Perkins's reaction might be. I need not have worried. 'It's an insult,' he cried ferociously, 'But it will sell the book'.

In 1980 came a radical revision of the whole Anglican Liturgy with the appearance of the Alternative Service Book.

There were some who felt that Westminster Abbey, as a Royal Peculiar and therefore having a very real independence, could well carry on with its liturgical round unaffected by ASB. The Dean of Westminster, Dr Eric Abbott, as Ordinary, how-ever, wisely decided even when the ASB was in its early and experimental stage that this would be wrong, and that Westminster Abbey just could not ignore what was happening in the *Ecclesia Angl-icana* as a whole. As a result of this decision, implemented progressively across the years, the Abbey may reasonably claim to have secured the best of both worlds. It still uses 1662 for its daily sung Evensongs, for its said early Communion on Saints' Days in Henry VII's Chapel, and in the Nave at 8 a.m. on Sunday. The Alternative Service Book is used daily (Rite B) for the said early Communion and at midday (Rite A). As for the offices of baptism and marriage, these are a matter of choice to be discussed with parents and those entering into matrimony. What kind of language ought to be used in a modern liturgy remains a matter of debate. Certainly it needs to be subtly evocative at different levels of human experience as in poetry. To trivialize in such a building as the Abbey must be wrong.

The decision to use the Alternative Service Book (Rite B) for the Sung Eucharist has had the effect of making the 'Perkins' way of doing things, already beginning to lose its coherence, need radical reform. Many of the existing liturgical movements when applied to ASB ceased to have meaning. After much discussion and experiment-ation, a new ceremonial has been worked out. Though constant changes in liturgy are not help-ful, for they sap confidence and make one too conscious of the mechanics, yet fixity for too long, when psychological and spiritual responses change, has equal dangers. What is needed at the Abbey, and Dr Perkins in his generation had it in large doses, is certainly sensitivity to the building.

However, worship provided in the Abbey is by no means confined to 1662 and ASB. If it were so, this Collegiate Church would not fully discharge the ministry which, in its unique situation, it is in a position to offer. I am not thinking only of great national occasions or royal events. The Abbey has progressively come to recognize that it has another mission, and has endeavoured to discharge it with all the compromises and ambiguities which this entails. This was particularly seen when Westminster Abbey in 1965/6 celebrated the nine-hundredth anniversary of its foundation. The Dean and Chapter, together with members of the staff, recognized that they must look outwards – the Abbey has no diocese to look to – as well as inwards, and that they must not be content, as in 1760, to sing Matins and Evensong and enjoy a comfortable dinner in College Hall. For twelve months, taking as their theme 'One People', they sought to find out, and identify the Abbey with all those of whatever faith – or of none – who in a world of fratricidal strife and travail of spirit were bearing witness to the undying hope that 'Earth shall be free and all her people one'. This process of identification meant special services, lectures, musical events, fun and games, ecumenical gatherings and contacts which transcended the divisions of race, creed, colour and culture. In this process the Abbey, rooted in Christian faith, acted as host. Also it was agreed that though the tempo could not, indeed ought not, be maintained, yet the thrust and the theme must go on – as it still does. Thus the contacts then made, the societies and institutions to whom we stretched out the hands of fellowship – and they to us – for the most part continue as new challenges emerge.

In particular, the special services have become a marked feature of the Abbey's worshipful life, varying as they do in character and scope. Some are extremely simple and are held in the Nave, relating to contemporary issues such as War on Want, the United Nations and the plight of dissidents whose conscience makes them captives. Many national societies now come to the Abbey to mark worshipfully an anniversary; others come annually as, for example, nurses, guides and scouts on which occasions the Abbey is bursting at the seams with young people. Many services have a family as well as a national interest. The service for the legal profession at the opening of the Michaelmas Term at which judges and barristers are there in force, is a case in point – it is encouraging to see a steady increase in the number of women amongst these. The Lord Chancellor comes in his full regalia and reads a lesson chosen by himself. It is the one occasion when the time taken to usher the large congregation into their seats is longer than the service itself. In the quest for appropriate hymns I can recall the Lord Chancellor helping me by singing part of 'Rock of Ages cleft for me' in a Latin translation by Gladstone. These services are drawn up by Abbey personnel getting round a table with those who have requested them, each side contributing from its own experience to the final form – the ultimate responsibility rests with the Dean as Ordinary. What would seem to be appropriate and is effective elsewhere can on occasions fall flat in the Abbey. All such services need to have something unique, usually a high personal content.

Some of our special services have a distinctively moving quality about them, not easily accounted for, others not to the same degree. The memorial service for Ernest Bevin had its own éclat when the miners from Wales turned up in large numbers and almost brought the roof down with their singing of 'Cwm Rhondda'. Whatever the purists may say, and they don't lack 'vocality', people like to sing. At the level of releasing a common popular emotion this is a way of securing a sense of personal involvement. At the sung statutory services in the Choir we invite the congregation to associate themselves silently with the objective worship being offered on their behalf and in their presence. This is right, and such services, to quote what I have said earlier, are essential to the rhythm of our daily worship – its heart-beat. But we have to accept that this will not minister to all of the people for whom we have a responsibility when they come to the Abbey. People attend acts of worship here who would seldom be seen in their own parish church or local congregation. Some have called the efforts to minister to them pandering to 'folk religion'. If by this is meant an endeavour to explore deeply into fundamental human experience and encourage this to express itself worshipfully, is anything wrong in this? I believe it was F. D. Maurice, whose bust is in St George's

Chapel at the west end of the Nave, who was the first to coin the phrase 'religionless Christianity'. He maintained that it is in ordinary, everyday experience as we seek to respond to the challenges of being alive as people that we shall find the spirit of God already at work within us. To illustrate this he affirmed that a man who takes a pig-sty and converts it into a home for his wife and family is engaged in a highly religious act. He is seeking to lift their corporate life into a higher and more personal dimension.

Surely there is a precedent here for what the Abbey is seeking to do which goes back for centuries. The monks sang their offices in the Choir: but there were many people milling around the Nave and threading their way through to the Shrine, who were then caught up in a more popular cultus. The Shrine was not the end, but might well prove the beginning of something stirring in the depths of their consciousness. Particularly important in our ministry at the Abbey is the one minute of prayer, relayed over the whole building, every hour throughout the day.

I have said little so far of the Sacrament of the Word, but this does not mean that it is unimportant. Both Charter and Statutes make it abundantly clear that the Dean and Chapter are required to exercise a teaching ministry through lectures and sermons. Indeed, they appoint a *lector theologiae* whose responsibility it is to organize courses of lectures, particularly in Advent and Lent. The present *lector theologiae* presides over the Jerusalem Chamber Society inaugurated by his predecessor. Lunch-time services sometimes contain addresses on set themes. The 'One People Oration' makes it possible for well-known people with deep personal commitments to share them with a largish audience in the Abbey. The bookshop helps the Dean and Chapter to fulfil their trust to educate and inform. This is important at a time when many thoughtful and good people feel that they cannot make a full assent to Christian Faith while at the same time preserving their intellectual integrity. To minister folk religion is certainly *not* the only duty of Westminster Abbey, though, as I have suggested, it is an important one. This Collegiate Church has behind it a long tradition of scholarship being kept alive by those who are or have recently been members of the Chapter.

Lectures and books are important because there are certain limitations involved in respect of the Abbey pulpit. Many distinguished preachers from the Chapter have occupied it – Lancelot Andrewes, South, Atterbury, Buckland, Stanley, Henson, Charles, Gore and Temple, to mention but a few. Also preachers from all over the Anglican Communion and of all denominations have 'uttered' here. Sometimes preachers have used the Abbey pulpit to propagate and commend their views on Church and State – and there is nothing improper in this.

One great limitation which used to be inherent in the Abbey pulpit has now been overcome. I refer to audibility. 'How can they hear without a preacher?' asks St Paul. But the trouble at the Abbey used to be that we had the preacher but people could not hear him. Before an effective

Sir Thomas Bromley, heart-broken after presiding over the trial of Mary Queen of Scots. He himself died soon after. He is depicted with six of his eight sons and daughters.

sound system was introduced into the Abbey it must have been quite impossible to make the human voice audible from the pulpit in the Crossing except to those in the Choir and the privileged in the front rows of the Transepts. As to the Nave, except when preaching from Cranmer's pulpit, audibility was out of the question.

But certain limitations of a different order still remain. It is not easy for the preacher to be intimate and personal – and not to feel that the building frustrates his efforts. A closely reasoned argument does not easily get over. The congregation is a mixed one on Sundays, and for many of them it may well be the only day when they will ever enter the Abbey. Their standard of education and cultural backgrounds are obviously different. Also they may have been caught up in the service 'unawares' and cannot, without embarrassment, escape. What is essential is that the preacher penetrates into living human experience.

For preaching the Nave has many advantages over the Choir. It is an enclosure and the preacher is visible to all. It is here that the evening congregational services fostered by Stanley, in spite of opposition, are held. As it was the Dean of the time who inaugurated them, so he still chooses the preacher and conductor. This service makes possible courses of addresses, and is helped by a simple, uncomplicated order.

As to Sunday preaching the canonical members of the Chapter have their terms of three months' residence during the course of the year, the usual custom being for the Canon to preach at either the morning (10.30 a.m.) or afternoon service (3 p.m.) and to invite a preacher for the other. It is not an easy assignment for a visitor, clergyman or layman, since the temptation is to put his 'all' into the address, the result too often being disastrous. Nor is a Hibbert lecture required. On the whole, however, our visitors do well.

FIVE

A Royal Peculiar

By AD 1100 the Abbey owned more than 11,000 acres of land, forty being around the Abbey. To add to its responsibilities the community were Lords of the manor of Westminster and this in itself not only meant courts and jurisdiction but a special link with the Crown. As a mitred churchman, the Abbot of Westminster sat in the Upper House of Parliament. Thus the location of the monastery of Westminster, living its life cheek by jowl with the Royal Palace, the judiciary and Parliament introduced another and distinctive element into its corporate life. Even had there been a wish to do so, the monastery could not have clinically immunized itself from what was going on around it. Conversely, the monarch must inevitably be concerned with the life of this uniquely situated monastery, particularly in the choice of its Abbot even to overriding the electoral powers of the monks and using his influence behind the scenes. It mattered that a monastery boasting a monarchical foundation and housing the Shrine of the saintly Confessor should not be hostile to or non-cooperative with the policy of the Crown. For this reason it was important that the Abbey be independent of any episcopal jurisdiction, whether of the Archbishop of Canterbury or of the Bishop of London. This Henry III secured. Equally it was necessary for St Edward's monastery to be exempted from the jurisdiction of the Provincial of the Benedictine Order. This also happened and the monastery came directly under the Pope.

Thus throughout the Middle Ages the Abbey held a 'peculiar' position as far as jurisdiction and its relations with the Crown were concerned. So it was that when monasteries were dissolved by law under Henry VIII and the Abbey became first a Cathedral Church, then after a brief return to a Benedictine monastery under Mary, a Collegiate Church, Queen Elizabeth specifically created her-

Phillippa, Duchess of York, held the lordship of the Isle of Wight after her husband was slain at the Battle of Agincourt.

self its Visitor and released it as before from any form of episcopal control. She herself as Supreme Governor of the Church of England took over from the Pope, jurisdiction being finally vested in her own person. Under her the Dean exercised his authority as Ordinary and the Dean and Chapter fulfilled the Trust vested in them. Still today when a new Archbishop of Canterbury (or sometimes a Bishop of London, but not of late) is appointed to his office he comes along with his legal official to Jerusalem Chamber where the Dean and Chapter meet him with their legal secretary. A protest is then solemnly read which says in effect that the Archbishop has no rights, jurisdiction or pre-

cedence in the Abbey but enters it only at the invitation of the Dean. Once read, the protest is solemnly witnessed and signed. Of late the acerbity of this legal admonition has been softened but its substance remains. I think it was Archbishop Coggan who, hearing this screed read, remarked with his accustomed courtesy and good humour: 'We are not amused.'

Let it be said that of late relations of this Royal Peculiar to the Primates of All England are excellent both at the personal and official levels. They come often to the Abbey for royal, national and synodical occasions, also for consecration of bishops, and are always welcome.

Is this protest, you may well ask, merely a piece of antiquarian, olde worlde mumbo-jumbo of no practical import or contemporary significance such as ecclesiastics too often delight in? The answer is 'no'. What this document does is to maintain and safeguard for the Abbey a real measure of independence from the normal channels of authority within the Church of England.

This is a treasured inheritance of contemporary relevance and must not be whittled away.

This independence, or isolation, means, for example, that if any member of the Collegiate Body of the Church of St Peter in Westminster feels himself aggrieved he can appeal to the Sovereign as Visitor who will then refer the matter to the Lord Chancellor. It is then up to him to make a judgement and report back to the Visitor who implements it if he or she thinks fit. The aggrieved cannot run off to any archbishop or bishop and should he do so is automatically referred back to the Dean.

When I came to the Abbey there was a very unhappy dispute, which had rankled for years, between the Dean and Chapter on the one hand and the minor canons with some officers of the College on the other. (I was very relieved that it was over before I arrived.) Finally, this *contretemps* was taken to the Visitor through the initiative of the latter party and was passed on to the Lord Chancellor. As a result Lord Simmonds sat with

two eminent colleagues and the matter was argued out thoroughly and evidence taken, each side being represented by counsel. It was all a very sad affair but, alas, when corporate bodies have internal problems which they cannot settle within their own institution there is no alternative but resort to some objective authority with power to decide. Such is the role, at Westminster Abbey, of the Visitor.

The result of the hearing held in the Privy Council offices was a Supplemental Charter which abolished freehold tenure for some officers of the College and the minor canons. At least this judgement in one sense removed ambiguity but left behind it broken human relations and much frustration. Fortunately time, the sensitivity of the Dean, Alan Don, and an overriding loyalty to the Abbey finally brought healing. Now this adjudication is a 'long forgotten far-off thing' and one of many 'battles long ago'. The constitutional decision then made is still operative. I can only recall one remark of Mr Justice Simmonds as recorded in the official report on the proceedings. It runs as follows: 'How long am I to be afflicted with this gossip, and tittle-tattle?'

To complete this story it must be added that the Dean and Chapter, on their own initiative, approached the Visitor for permission in future to break the freehold in respect of any subsequent member of Chapter and to fix seventy years as a retiring age.

But there is much more to the status of independence than the somewhat negative one of dealing with redress of grievances. Some years ago the Church of England in its elective assembly declared itself against what are known as 'Inter-Faith' services. The most prominent and publicized of such occasions being the Commonwealth Inter Faith Observance attended by the Queen. The first of these was held at the Church of St Mary le Bow when Joseph McCulloch was Rector. It then moved to St Martin-in-the-Fields. However, after the Church of England had expressed its negative view the Vicar there, Austen Williams, felt, very understandably though most reluctantly, that he ought not to hold this annual observance at St Martin's. It was then transferred to the Guild-hall – a 'desacralization', as many regarded it. After a few years the Dean and Chapter were given to understand that the Queen would welcome its being taken over by the Abbey. This is precisely what has happened and it is now regarded as a most

significant event in the annual calendar. Long may it remain so.

In taking this step of being a host church the Abbey is not committing the Church of England, as such, to anything. The Dean as Ordinary, in this case Eric Abbott, was exercising a proper constitutional authority vested in him under a Royal Charter. Before making his decision the Dean consulted the Chapter who were entirely in favour, Canon Max Warren, a former General Secretary of the Church Missionary Society, expressing this view strongly.

This is an excellent example of the utility, on occasions, of the Abbey's independence. It means that the Collegiate Church is as free as it has the courage to be. However, this freedom can only be justified if it is used responsibly and sometimes with restraint. If it is frivolously deployed it could become an abuse and its right to exist would be weakened.

I can think of many services held in the Abbey which must have led to a degree of criticism. However, if any complaint were to reach the Archbishop of Canterbury in relation to them or to any event at the Abbey, he would be able to disclaim responsibility for what had happened. Indeed he would be perfectly free in replying to a complainant, while pointing this out, to give his own views – and this he could do without any embarrassment to the Abbey.

One service I well remember, since it seemed to me especially significant, was a Sung Eucharist on 21 January 1984, to 'celebrate the fortieth anniversary of the Reverend Florence Li Tim Oi, the first woman to be ordained priest in the Anglican communion'. The background to this ordination was the war in China, the desperate need for Bishop Hall of Hong Kong to add to his staff and the fruitful ministry of Florence Li Tim Oi as a deacon. In this extreme situation and isolated in China, the Bishop made Florence a priest.

The Abbey Nave was crowded to capacity with, *inter alia,* deaconesses, licensed lay workers, and priests and deacons from other provinces. The Address was given by the Reverend Joyce M. Bennett ORC of Hong Kong and Macao. The Archbishop of Canterbury sent to Florence Li Tim Oi the following personal message which, with his permission, was read out by the Dean during the Service:

A glimpse of King Henry VII's Chapel – as beautiful without as within.

Dear Florence Li Tim Oi

It is with a deep sense of gratitude for your Christian witness and ministry that I send greetings to you on the 40th anniversary of your ordination to the priesthood.

I know from recent conversations with many Christians in China that over the intervening years you have maintained a steady and single-minded devotion to Our Lord and his Church. Often you have had to work under difficult and tragic circumstances. Sometimes you have suffered from misunderstandings about your ministry. You have never been eager to promote yourself but only to build up the life of the Church and serve its mission in places of desperate human need.

Your selfless ministry is an example to us all.

On this very special day for you, I thank God for all that you have been to so many people. I rejoice that you are still exercising your ministry within our own Anglican family and I pray that you may have many more active years in the service of the One Lord we both strive to serve in the fellowship of the Church.

This was surely well said.

Another special service, equally moving but of a very different order, was the occasion when some eight hundred guide dogs with their blind owners were present in the Nave. I hope, one day, this will find its way into *The Guinness Book of Records*.

There are many benefits resulting from the Abbey's status as a Royal Peculiar. There are certain leaders of the world religions – I deplore the term 'non-Christian' since to define in terms of negatives is, to say the least, discourteous – who come to the Abbey, as British citizens, and would not find it so easy to attend functions in other church buildings. This is particularly true of some members of the Jewish community. The Abbey is a national church, as perhaps no other church is, with all the ambiguities, challenges and opportunities which this opens up.

Benefits and 'spin-offs' are fine but sometimes they go along with disadvantages or what at first sight may seem to be so. One of these, in respect of Westminster Abbey, is that financially it must paddle its own canoe. Unlike cathedral bodies it receives no grants from the Church Commissioners nor would they bale it out if it overspent and went into the red. The Dean and Chapter and our talented head lay administrator, the former Receiver General, therefore recognized the need for advice and help in certain specialized areas. Panels were set up relating to architectural matters, investment and the sound system as well as other smaller committees. These have proved invaluable and the Abbey is fortunate in attracting such high-level support so freely given.

The status of being a Royal Peculiar has further and more subtle effects upon those who are members of the corporate body. True, 'No man is an Island, entire of it self' and that is certainly true of Westminster Abbey. But equally true is the fact that we have no diocesan loyalty, no bishop to look to. Until recently Deans of Westminster were *ex-officio* members of the Synod, though now they must seek election to that body if they wish to participate in its deliberations. Hence the overriding need for the Abbey to prevent any excessive, myopic preoccupation with its own affairs. There is a very real world outside the Precinct's wall.

SIX

Community and College

WE LIKE to think of our Abbey family as consisting of those who in the past or in the present have had close associations with this church. The number must approximate to some six hundred.

The original community goes back, certainly in embryo, to AD 1049 and survived *in situ* until 1540 when it was dissolved by Act of Parliament under Henry VIII, who converted the Abbey into the Cathedral Church of the new diocese of Westminster. This proved to be as short-lived as did its revival as a monastery under Queen Mary. Finally her half-sister, Queen Elizabeth, created the Collegiate Church of St Peter in Westminster by giving it, and also Westminster School, a Charter in 1560. It has remained as such, apart from the sixteen years of the Commonwealth, until today. Thus the Abbey was a Benedictine monastery for nearly 500 years, and has been for over four centuries, a collegiate church.

The life of the Abbey family, therefore, begins with the Benedictine monks. Members of the two communities, monastery and college, in their differing ways, professed and called themselves Christian; both have found the locus of their worship in a prestigious building on Thorney Island; both communities have used the same 'plant', occupying for varying purposes the same houses; both have had responsibilities for the manor and later the City of Westminster; both have been caught up in royal and national events into which they have introduced a religious dimension. When the Ampleforth monks returned to sing Vespers in the Abbey Choir (see p.69) this was far more than a conventional response to a fraternal invitation. They had long memories. It was a happy thought on the part of the Very Reverend Michael Mayne, in his address when recently installed as Dean of Westminster, to recall this significant inheritance. For some five hundred years, he said, the Abbey had been the home of a Benedictine community and he would wish to see the ancient tradition of a common life in Christ and of warmth and hospitality maintained.

The head of the community was the Abbot. He was elected by the Chapter as a whole, though the process could on occasion be somewhat complicated. There was the possibility that the King would intervene, in which case the election was only nominally a free one. The Abbot was usually chosen from amongst those who had already held the office of Prior and who, since the Abbot was frequently on the move, was often in charge of affairs at Westminster. Once elected, he was in theory expected to undertake the expensive and often dangerous journey to Rome to secure papal confirmation, though this was later commuted into a money payment more or less equivalent to the cost of a personal visit. He was treated with respect and deference. A monk passing him in the monastery would acknowledge him with a low bow. In the early days, however, no provision was made for his separate accommodation which meant that he would sleep in the dormitory and dine regularly with the monks in the refectory. In the process of time the duties and responsibilities of his office increased steadily. His share of the monastic properties was hived off from that of the Convent generally. His personal need to entertain and offer hospitality, sometimes to the monarch, grew, which necessitated a house sufficiently large for him to play the host in some style. This was therefore provided, thanks to Nicholas Litlyngton and, on the eve of the Dissolution, by John Islip. Thus the Abbot ended up with palatial accommodation which included numerous bedrooms, a dining-hall with a minstrels' gallery, and Jerusalem Chamber which served as a large 'withdrawing'-room. The Abbot had his own staff of servants, and separate financial accountancy.

His position was by no means an easy one, for his growing differentiation from the day-to-day life of the community meant that there were tensions

Vestibule to the very fine Chapter House, completed and in use by 1269.

rising from conflicts of interest or of personality. Mistakes were made in his appointment, as William the Conqueror found. This dilemma is well illustrated in the racy narrative of the Chronicle of Jocelin of Brakelond, *circa* 1200, concerning the events of his day at the distinguished Benedictine monastery of St Edmund. The community there was surprisingly similar to Westminster with its shrine and royal connections. Jocelin contrasts the two Abbots of his own day.

Abbot Hugh was grown old and his eyes waxed somewhat dim. Pious he was and kindly, a strict monk and good but in the business of this world neither good nor wise. Discipline and religion and all things pertaining to the rule were regularly observed within the cloister but outside all things were badly handled and everyone did as he pleased.... The Abbey woods were destroyed, the houses of its meadows threatened to fall into ruin and day by day all things went from bad to worse. The Abbot had but one remedy and one consolation to borrow money.

Abbot Sansom, however, was a different kettle of fish, for he thought more highly of good administration than of maintaining the discipline of the monastic life.

This Abbot seems to love the active life better than the contemplative life. He had more praise for good obedientiaries than for good cloister monks and rarely did he approve of any man solely for his knowledge of literature unless he were also wise in worldly affairs, and when he heard of any prelate ... turned anchorite, he did not praise him for so doing. He was loth to bestow much praise on kindly men, for he said, 'He that seeks to please everyone, ought to please nobody'.

There was needed a man of experience, of tact and firmness, whom the community could respect and who would build bridges rather than himself contribute to division. Here, fortunately, the personal interest of the Conqueror in this Abbey church proved a long-term asset though it began rather unhappily. It was not a time, the Conqueror felt, when the electoral principle could be allowed 'unfettered' to apply and he himself made the first appointment. His choice fell on Geoffrey, Abbot of Jumièges, but this proved disastrous and William sent him packing back to Normandy in disgrace

Dark Cloister, or Kill-Canon-Corner. 'Blow, blow thou Winter wind, thou art not so unkind as man's ingratitude.'

after some five years of misrule. Prompted by Lanfranc, Archbishop of Canterbury, he next nominated Vitalis, Abbot of Bernay, to whom, as a sign of good will, the King conferred the grant of the manor of Doddington-with-Thorpe in Lincolnshire. His next appointment, Gilbert Crispin, once again prompted by Lanfranc, was an outstanding success, providing precisely what this young community needed. He was destined to hold the office for thirty-two years. His great achievement was to stabilize the convent, setting it properly on course.

The new Abbot was of noble birth, a scholar of international reputation and of a wide Christian charity who had worked with Lanfranc at Canterbury. He was also a prominent exponent of the need for monastic reform as epitomized in the Benedictine house at Bec which Gilbert had entered when a boy. He had travelled extensively, visiting universities in France and Italy, calling in at Rome and returning to Bec by way of Germany. Proof of the quality of his mind remains in his writings. These include a Life of Herluin, founder of Bec, and a Treatise on the Holy Spirit. Most interesting in the light of the modern dialogue of faiths is his *Disputation of a Jew with a Christian,* a discourse which a former Dean of Westminster, Armitage Robinson, has described as a 'controversial work of exceptional fairness'. Indeed so temperate was Gilbert that he was attacked by a contemporary for 'leaning' towards his opponent.

Crispin's reputation and church connections brought the convent at Westminster into the wider ecclesiastical world of the Continent. Thus he and the community were involved in a Council which was held in St Catherine's Chapel in 1202. The Papal Legate was present and a decision was then made which decided definitively the long-continuing struggle for precedence between Canterbury and York. It did so by coming down in favour of the former as the Primate of All England and the latter as the Primate of England. A few years later Crispin participated in another Church Council which confirmed a settlement between the King and Archbishop Anselm on the vexed question of lay investiture.

So far as Westminster was concerned, the influence of Gilbert Crispin could be detected almost everywhere in the community's life. He went on with the building of the monastery; immersed himself in the management of its es-

tates; completed the building of the original Cloisters by 1100; and probably constructed the Abbot's first *camera* or lodgings.

Progressively, as the need arose across the years, some twenty monastic offices were created. From these the priors were usually elected and from the priors the abbots. As to the tenure and the holders of these offices, it may be illuminating to quote from a year taken at random, namely 1297/8 when Walter de Wenlok was Abbot. There were at that time 49 monks. Of these 20 never held any office at all; 12 held one; 5 two; 5 three; 5 four; 1 six and 1 seven. A hundred years later, when records were probably more reliable, the statistics in general present roughly the same picture. Perhaps we may rescue one monk whose career seems interesting, from oblivion.

Roger Cretton entered the monastery in 1384, though it was not until he had been there fourteen years that he began to be given administrative duties. Once embarked on this course, he was hardly ever without office during the next thirty-five years, becoming Treasurer, Kitchener, Cellarer, Granger, Warden of Queen Eleanor's and Richard II's manors, Warden of the Churches, Almoner, Infirmarer, Abbot's Receiver, and Sacrist. Even Archdeacon Pearce, in his *Monks of Westminster*, forsakes his customary *gravitas* to suggest slyly that it was 'appropriate' that he should die while conducting an audit. One wonders how he got on with his fellow monks or what they said about him behind his back.

Personal events in the life of the individual monk were of interest to the family as a whole. Grief and joys were shared. The four significant occasions in the life of a brother were his appearance as a junior; his first Mass, followed by a feast; his presiding in the Refectory, which meant sitting next to the Abbot and in his absence ringing the bell to call the community to order. Finally there was the monk's death and funeral.

The Order was not over-severe and the monks were released from any vow of poverty: indeed they received a 'rake-off' from the manorial rentals. From time to time it had become customary, at various periods in his conventual life, for a monk to receive a gift in kind which had a fixed monetary value. These presents were known as a 'regard', a 'refresher', a 'courtesy' or, more generally, '*exennia*'. They usually took the form of food and wine. As time went on these occasions grew more

frequent, additional gifts coming from the Warden of the Queen's manors and from the Infirmarer.

In the Chapter House, a magnificent building where the monks met to do business of various kinds, harsher punishments such as flogging were meted out, sometimes accompanied by confinement in one of the two prisons for lesser and greater crimes situated in Little Cloister.

Keeping warm during the winter, or often during a typical English summer, could never have been easy. There was then no Thames Embankment and the tide came sweeping in flushing the oyster beds in the monastic garden. The air was often damp by reason of mists rising from the Thames and its tributaries. There was no effective heating within the Abbey and the monks trooping into the Choir for their night offices must have shivered as they sang. The only communal place where a fire was usually kept burning was in the Undercroft where general chat and conversation was the order of the day and, maybe, off-the-record discussion of Chapter business.

What about their health? Fortunately, owing to the researches of Lord Amulree, himself a medical

The Norman Undercroft (LEFT). Here the medieval monks who suffered and shivered from the damp and mists of Thorney Island, are endeavouring to keep warm.

The Chapter Office, Dean's Yard, originally the cellarer's House, now the administrative headquarters of the Abbey.

man, we are able to answer this question in some detail. As was the rule in all monasteries, the Abbey had an infirmary to care for monks who through illness were unable to take their place in Choir. On entry, a sick monk brought with him his own bed; the Infirmarer also kept a number of flock and feather cushions for the comfort of more long-term patients. In the common dormitory the monk would have a straw mattress, blanket, coverlet and pillow. At Westminster Abbey the customary Infirmarer's hall was part of a small cloister, the ill monks having rooms opening off it. At the east end of the cloister was the Chapel of St Catherine. The Infirmarer was not himself a doctor, his responsibilities being largely administrative, though he was expected to be 'gentle, good tempered, kind, compassionate to the sick, and willing to gratify their needs with affectionate sympathy.... He should provide in a spirit of fraternal sympathy a fire on the hearth should the state of the weather require it, a candle or a cresset, and a lamp to burn all night.' As an administrator he kept strict accounts and received money from Abbey properties to run the Infirmary.

The Westminster records refer to 706 patients of whom 484 were received into the Infirmary at one time or another, the average age of a monk at his death being about fifty-one years. The main preoccupation of the Infirmarer was with a small group of monks, about one third of the patients, whose health broke down at regular intervals. The longest stay recorded in the infirmary was one of seven years!

From 1296 to 1536 some eighty-nine monks were submitted to elementary surgery. As to methods of treatment, resort was made to cuppings and administrations of clysters, sometimes on the advice of a physician. Other treatments were part of a normal routine – electuaries, oxymels, cholagogues, and ointments – and could be laid on from the Infirmary's own store. Here the herb garden was essential. Male nurses were included on the staff, and they were particularly bidden 'to endure the foulness of such persons whether in vomitting or other matters'. From the thirteenth century it was not uncommon to call in a doctor from outside, though in 1320 Master Robert of St Alban's was appointed to the monastery in this capacity on a stipend of 53s 4d per year. This office continued right up to the Dissolution, though those holding it remain rather shadowy figures.

Two of them were Oxford graduates and royal physicians to Richard II and Henry IV, the health of the latter being for some time before his death seriously in decline. Feminists will be pleased to hear that one of the doctors was a woman, '*mulier fisicus*', who was often called in to see patients and was paid the usual fees. Apparently women doctors were not exceptional at this time.

A monastery living its life in the heart of a Westminster increasingly becoming a centre of government could not have found it easy to isolate itself from national affairs. Regular royal occasions, coronations and the like, were bound to generate an atmosphere which could easily envelop the community as they still do today.

In all that happened at Westminster Abbey during the five hundred years of its existence, no event lowered its prestige more than the notorious robbery of 24 April 1303. That this could have taken place at all was due to the monastery's sad state of decline. The enthusiasm engendered by Henry III's rebuilding had waned; Edward I was away in the North; Abbot de Wenlock was old and infirm. The result was that some monks ran amok.

The scene moves to the Low Countries where there resided a certain Richard Puddlicott who abandoned the tonsure for the more lucrative gains of a wool merchant. In Ghent he was suddenly imprisoned as a hostage for Edward I's unredeemed debts. He managed to escape and fled in penury to London where he haunted Westminster Hall, 'but no man gave unto him'. In desperation he succeeded in stealing, undoubtedly with collusion from within, the entire stock of silver from the Refectory on which he lived for a few months. He then, with great daring, managed to steal the whole of the King's treasure from the crypt under the Chapter House, possibly with the help of the Sacrist, all this being worth £100,000, equivalent to a year's state revenue. For a time nothing happened until a fisherman netted a silver goblet in the Thames and other booty was found. One woman of loose living accounted for her possession of a precious ring by alleging it was given her by the Sacrist, 'so that she should become his friend'.

At last the King was apprised of these events and returned immediately to London. He was not amused. Puddlicott was arrested; the Abbot and forty-eight monks were sent to the Tower; six laymen were hanged. Some ten monks remained in the Tower but when the King returned finally

David Cranfield, first Earl of Middlesex, on whose tomb this magnificent, fearsome griffin is squatting, had a meteoric rise to greatness but the same power that made him – the Duke of Buckingham – broke him.

from the North, flushed with victory over the Scots, he preferred not to risk a conflict with the Church over 'benefit of clergy' and they were released. Puddlicott, who accepted full responsibility – he cannot have been telling the truth – pleaded his 'orders' in vain and, two years after his crime, was hanged. The chronicler of Westminster Abbey accepted Puddlicott's impossible story thus maintaining that the monks were wholly innocent, and in this he was supported by other monasteries.

We have seen how in the early days of the Benedictine monastery of Westminster, just when stability and firm guidance were needed, William the Conqueror and Lanfranc found these qualities in Abbot Gilbert. It is a curious coincidence that as the sands of time were running out for the monastery, some four hundred years later another Abbot who won universal respect led the convent for some thirty-two years, that is from 27 October 1500 to 12 May 1532. I refer to John Islip, and in doing so reluctantly pass over many others of solid worth. Undoubtedly he was among the Abbey's greatest rulers.

John Islip, who incidentally spelt his own name in twelve different ways, was almost certainly a member of the family of Archbishop Simon Islip. He was born on 10 June 1464 and entered the community on St Benedict's Day, 21 March 1480. His administrative gifts soon manifested themselves and he held a whole gamut of offices, some sixteen in all, ending up with his becoming Prior in 1498. He almost immediately set out on an extensive tour of the manors and became involved in the

abortive attempt to secure the body of Henry VI for burial in the Abbey rather than its going to either Chertsey or Windsor. He was appointed Abbot Estney's Receptor, until on the latter's death the almost inevitable happened and he became Abbot, being installed on 25 November 1500. He could hardly have entered into this office at a worse time, certainly not financially. There were royal subsidies to be met and a 5 per cent tax to be paid on monastic offices. Income from the Shrine was decreasing and offerings at various altars had dropped alarmingly. Islip made the bold decision not to economize – in fact he enlarged expenditure – but to increase income. Doubtless he had a prophetic intimation of those wise, but often neglected, words of Mr Micawber! Rents from Abbey properties were raised; receipts from Henry VII's Coronation and his mother's funeral helped to swell funds. Abbot Islip cooperated with the King in the building of Henry VII's Chapel, himself laying the foundation stone. Churchman and monarch became friends and the latter was occasionally entertained in the Abbot's lodgings. The King, on his part, sent the Abbot two tuns of wine every year, which, considering his parsimonious character, was a tribute indeed. Islip was never as intimate with his successor, though he may have been in part instrumental in securing better terms from Henry VIII for the Abbey than were meted out to other monasteries. The royal confidence in the Abbot may be seen in his appointing John Islip treasurer of the Savoy Hospital which was then in process of being built. During Islip's first Christmas in office the Prior, monks, bailiff and all the convent, dined with the Lord Abbot in his manor at Neyte.

One important change in the internal life of the community which began under his predecessor, Abbot George Fascet, was further exploited by John Islip and must have led to comment and maybe criticism. As Abbot he seems to have taken the management of the monastery very largely into his own hands. From his installation he acted as Sacrist and Warden of the New Work; also as Warden of the Lady Chapel. No longer was the burden of responsibility effectively spread among his brethren but he himself controlled the great spending departments. True, Thomas Jaye held from 1514 to 1528 the offices (not all at the same time) of Treasurer, Monk Bailiff, Warden of the Churches and of the Royal Manors and Cellarer.

The Chamber of the Pyx, where the standard pieces of gold and silver were kept.

Essential to an infirmary in a Benedictine monastery was the chapel with its altar. Healing was a divine work and there were prayers for the sick in St Catherine's Chapel (RIGHT).

When he became Prior in May 1525 these offices passed to the Abbot's Chaplain, John Fulwell, but he was thought to be equally the instrument of the Abbot. Archdeacon Pearce comments: 'In such a condition of things the greater part of the Brethren must have felt themselves to be mere cyphers in the administration of the House and the end was not far off.' Certainly the suggestion must be that Islip had scant confidence in many of his brethren.

The shape of things to come, a cloud as yet no bigger than a man's hand, was beginning to manifest itself. Although not yet fully linked up with an attack on papal jurisdiction, there was a movement, championed by Wolsey, for a degree of monastic reform. Here Wolsey had Islip's full support, and relations between the two were not difficult even when Islip received official notice from the Cardinal, in his capacity as Papal Legate, of a visitation of Westminster Abbey to take place on 10 January 1519. To this Islip replied courteously that he and his brethren, of whom he gave a list, would duly present themselves in the Chapter House on that day. No trace of what happened on this, or on any subsequent visitation, exists in the Abbey muniments. In addition to this use of his legatine powers Wolsey summoned all Benedictine abbots to meet him in Chapter at Westminster to discuss the reformation of their houses. There is a possibility that the Cardinal once more visited the convent of Westminster and imposed severe penalties upon it which were only relaxed as the result of a substantial bribe.

It was probably at this time that a document came into Polydore Vergil's hands, drawn up, so it was alleged, by a Westminster monk, which proved useful for the King's Commissioners on their visitation of the monasteries prior to their suppression. This *cri de cœur*, entitled 'A supplic-ation of a monk of Westminster to ye bishop of Rome', was written around the year 1518 when William Mane was Prior. The tale of woe that he unfolds is heartrending. The Prior, he maintained, had accused him of theft, which led him to take his complaint to the Abbot who advised that he should leave the matter in his hands. However, he did nothing and the ailing monk after a frightful attack of vomiting during his singing of the Mass was sent to the Infirmary where he remained some nine months and had to pay personally for his keep. Islip began to tire of this almost insoluble problem and in Chapter accused the complainant of being

'no more sick than his horse', a diagnosis which the outside doctors, whom our unhappy monk called in, doubtless mindful of their fees, entirely re-pudiated. Thus supported he made intercession for a papal bull to instruct the convent to appoint him to one of its benefices worth at least an annual income of £20; and at the same time to give him his 'portion' and a pension; also permission to retain his stall in the Choir and his voice in Chapter elections. As to the truth of the charges, together with the report of them which by some quirk of history has been preserved, we have no means of knowing; but they remind us of the difficulties, disputes and personal tensions which are bound to happen from time to time in such a small commun-ity whose individual members were called to live a fully corporate life. What Wolsey made of this *cri de cœur* we are equally ignorant of but it seems likely that this and other complaints which Islip in general admitted to the Cardinal led to a third visitation of the Abbey.

In large areas of life John Islip was caught up in secular business. Henry VIII soon recognized his capacity, making him a member of the Privy Council on the royal departure for France in 1518. He was also appointed a trier of petitions to Parliament and made a member of the Com-mission of Peace for Middlesex. He was asked by Wolsey to be a Commissioner for the affairs of the monastery at Gloucester and superintend a visit-ation of the Abbey of Malmesbury. Islip lived long enough to support, in a letter to the Pope, Henry VIII's divorce at Rome; and the King suggested to the curia that the Abbot, whom he describes as 'a good old father', should be an assessor to Arch-

bishop Warham for trying the cause of the divorce in England.

Such manifold and time-consuming concerns did not prevent his executing duties specifically associated with his office as Abbot. He raised the western towers up to the level of the roof; undertook a general repair of the church, in particular the buttresses; filled the niches with statues; and designed a central tower which he was forced to abandon because he found the pillars inadequate to take the weight. He enlarged the Abbot's House, and erected a gallery overlooking the Abbey on the south side.

John Islip was fortunate in not being directly involved in Wolsey's calamitous fall, but only the King's pardon for alleged minor offences and his 'offering' Henry nearby Abbey properties in return for more distant lands kept Islip safe and inviolate. The King's Exchequer benefited by two rich altar fronts of cloth of gold, powdered with scutcheons of the arms of Abbot Islip, and a cope of fine cloth of gold with a rich embroidery, with Islip's and other imagery.

Islip prepared a chantry chapel for the place of his burial where Masses were said at the two altars for the repose of his soul. A window by Hugh Easton in the upper chapel memorializes nurses killed in World War II.

It seems as if Islip is unique in that we probably know what he looked like in the flesh. The representation of him on the famous Islip Roll, that is the brief on which his death was to be announced to other monasteries, certainly suggests a personal portrait. It may be said that he represented the last of the great Abbots of Westminster at a time when the differentiation between Church and State, though coming, had not yet, in its fullness, arrived.

The monks were by no means the only class deeply involved in the day-to-day life of the Abbey. Besides them as members of the family there were the lay brethren, servants, and almsmen necessary to run a great institution, not forgetting those who looked after the horses or arranged for transport by river. Then there were functionaries who attended to the care and oversight of the manor of Westminster. The almsmen still survive and in their red cloaks are on view at Sunday services, looking very much like Chelsea Pensioners. They antedate the Reformation and are, perhaps, the oldest corporate body still at the Abbey. They were originally recruited as a bodyguard for the Abbot, now for the Dean, and are appointed personally on a warrant signed by the Sovereign.

The last few years at Westminster until the monastery was surrendered to the Crown on 16 January 1540 were, as one historian describes it, 'squalid'. Henry VIII took two bites at the cherry, suppressing the smaller monasteries – their inmates going into the larger, as happened later with theological colleges – until by a second Act all monasteries ceased. Of the forty-odd monks at Westminster some fifteen seem to have signed the deed of Dissolution, four of whom became prebendaries in the new cathedral which Henry VIII set up for a newly constituted diocese of Westminster; another four became lay-clerks, and four others went off to college as students. The setting up of a new cathedral, though it was somewhat curious to have two diocesan churches so close to each other, at least had the effect of preventing the Abbey being redundant as happened with some abbeys throughout the country. The church and also the domestic buildings remained.

As to the monks who left the Precincts, some were pensioned and paid off; some joined the new *Ecclesia Anglicana*; one (or it might be two) was faithful to his monastic vows and went over to France to fulfil them, thus giving birth, centuries later, to the Benedictine community at Ampleforth. For all members of the community it must have been an unsettling and strange experience. For those who continued haunting the old, familiar places, once rich in symbol and significance, their reaction might merit Shakespeare's words in another context: 'Bare ruin'd choirs, where late the sweet birds sang'.

The diocese of Westminster, never adequately endowed, did not last long; nor did the monastery revived by Queen Mary, perhaps the most tragic as she was the most religious of English monarchs. There seems no sure evidence as to the size of Mary's restored community, though it was probably about thirty-six. Perhaps it is significant that the last Abbot, John Feckenham, a man of great integrity who suffered much for his faith should have gone further than Islip and have entrusted the affairs of the monastery not to his brethren but to two laymen. The Receiver and the Auditor were the important people in the running of the house.

The dispersal of the community was the end of

*The ancient clock on the North West Tower (*LEFT*) strikes no more having given up its unequal struggle with Big Ben.*

an age. Henceforward over centuries the *Ecclesia Anglicana* and the Roman Catholic Church were to be cut off one from the other, theologically as well as socially, even when the latter was released from any legal disabilities. When I first came to Westminster Abbey, none of us, with the exception of one member of the Chapter, really knew anyone at Westminster Cathedral. (Our knowledge in practice was almost limited to the name of the Cardinal.) The first break-through was when Dean Alan Don escorted, 'darkly at dead of night', the Roman Catholic episcopal hierarchy into St Edward's Chapel, leaving them, as he put it, to pray for the Conversion of England.

Things are now quite different, not least because of the historic link that the Abbey has with the Ampleforth monks who still elect an Abbot of Westminster. Ampleforth possesses the only pre-Reformation Abbey cope in this country. The link here has increased since that never-to-be-forgotten day when Cardinal Hume, formerly Abbot of Ampleforth, brought his monks to sing Vespers in the Abbey on the day of his consecration as bishop in Westminster Cathedral. It was over four hundred years since the Benedictine Community had ceased to do so. No occasion could have been more poignant and as the Abbey clergy finally escorted the Cardinal down the central aisle there was a burst of spontaneous clapping which said everything. Afterwards we entertained the Ampleforth monks in what is now known as the Great Hall of Westminster School, but which used to be the dormitory of the Benedictine monks. The spirit of it all was relaxed, even loving, as we met together in fellowship. In a short speech I expressed a modicum of anxiety lest the monks, once returned to their old haunts, should stage a 'sit in', driving us to migrate along the road to the Cathedral in Victoria Street.

Some months later there was launched in the Throne Room of the Archbishop's house in Westminster – that impressive reminder of the *Im-*

perium Romanum – a recording of Cardinal Hume's consecration and enthronement together with the singing of Vespers in the Abbey. The Cardinal spoke, I spoke, and then the lovable and non-pompous Duke of Norfolk concluded the speeches. 'The Reformation,' he began, 'was a load of rubbish!' A gasp went round the Throne Room. Then he repeated it. 'The Reformation was a load of rubbish! The Cecils got all the land and the Howards lost their heads.' Here, certainly, potted family history became alive and contemporary.

It seemed singularly fitting that not long after this event Cardinal Hume paid another visit to the Abbey with the Archbishop of Canterbury, the moderator of the General Assembly of the Church of Scotland, and the moderator of the Free Church Federal Council. The purpose was to unveil a plaque close to the tomb of Queen Mary and her half-sister Queen Elizabeth, in memory of all those who, at the time of the Reformation, gave up their lives for Christ and conscience' sake.

Margaret, Countess of Lennox, whose beauty universally charmed, was a daughter of the widow of James IV of Scotland, niece to Henry VIII and grandmother of James I through her son's, Lord Darnley's, marriage to Mary Queen of Scots. She consorted with kings and queens but died in poverty.

SEVEN

'The Old Order Changeth Yielding Place to New'

THE CLOSURE of the Convent on the accession of Elizabeth made it certain that whatever religious institution followed it would not be another monastery. The Queen herself had never conformed under Mary and she was known to be a Protestant as well as a *politique*. The result was the setting up of the Collegiate Church of St Peter in Westminster by a Charter dated 1560.

What kind of Church did this document envisage? The Charter reads curiously in its constant repetition, but its main intention was clear, namely to replace the Pope by the Sovereign, and to invest the newly constituted Dean and Chapter with the church and the properties hitherto held by the monastery. Queen Mary is described as 'our dear sister' without further comment but the reference to the former Westminster monks is far from flattering. The Charter makes it clear that though the Queen acts out of 'mere motion' the Collegiate Church's existence derives from an Act of Parliament which, after dissolving the monasteries, put them in the hands of the Crown. In doing this the purpose was to bring 'true religion and worship' back to their 'original and natural sincerity', after correcting 'the enormities to which the life and professions of the monks had for long lapsed and which so disgracefully proliferated there'. This was not a fair comment when applied to Westminster. The influence of a Benedictine past is seen not only in the Sovereign replacing the Pope but also in releasing the Abbey from any archepiscopal or episcopal jurisdiction; in the constitutional status of the Dean as Ordinary; and in the continued possession of the Abbey estates, though reduced, and dispersed throughout the country.

More interesting than the Charter, in spite of their limited legality, are the Statutes since they provide a clear indication of the 'life style' which it was hoped would obtain at the Abbey. The new Collegiate Church is to continue as a community. It is not to be the kind of institution in which the individuals who comprise it go their separate ways. All the officers of the establishment, and they are many, come under the authority of the Dean or the Dean and Chapter with appeal to the Queen as Visitor. The Statutes define explicitly what is required in respect of the various members of the College. Thus out of twelve prebendaries four are expected always to be present at services and any break in this observance will lead to a fine. There is to be a common table, with a scale of charges, open to all members of the Collegiate body, who must seek permission for any absenteeism. There is provision for a head and second cook, a head and second butler, two valets, a chamberlain, a cup bearer, a miller, a porter who is also a barber, a groom, a laundress, a servant for cleaning water pipes and roofs of the church. These are resident with board and lodging.

What is remarkable in these Statutes is their amazing detail, particularly where it relates to the boys at either of the two schools:

Faces and hands shall be washed, hair combed and cut, nails cut, linen and woollen garments, outer garments, boots and shoes shall be kept clean and polished, so that no lice or dirt shall infect them or their fellow scholars. They shall not go outside the precincts of the College without leave.... After prayers they shall make their beds. Then each one shall sweep out the dust and filth from under his bed into the middle of the room; four of them, appointed by the prefect, shall sweep the various small piles of dirt into a single heap and remove it from the room.

In one respect, though not in all, an intention implicit in the Statutes was never fulfilled and this was mainly due to the advent of a married clergy. A Benedictine monastery was an exclusively male affair and apart from the 'laundress' there is no reference to women in the Statutes, though some of the servants were certainly of this sex. Elizabeth, as we know, had a strong prejudice against married clergymen and is reported to have said to her host Mrs Whitgift when visiting the Archbishop at Lambeth: 'Madame I may not call you, Mistress I dare not call you – but I thank you.'

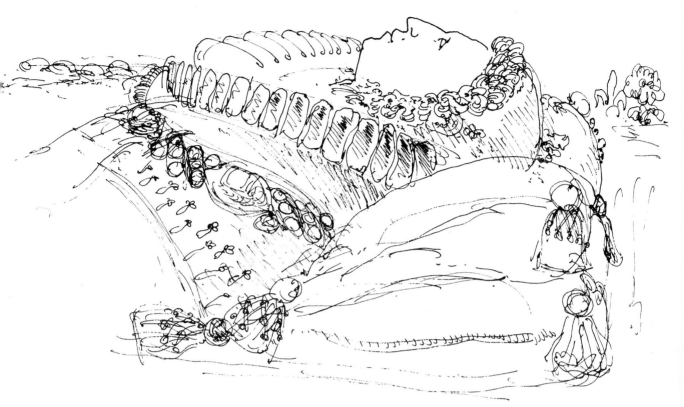

Queen Elizabeth was the second founder of Westminster Abbey. She is well described on her tomb, where she is buried with Mary her half-sister, as 'The mother of this her country, the nurse of religion and learning, renowned for her skill in many languages, a prince incomparable'.

The effect of married prebendaries was an increasing inclination on their part to desert the common table and to feed in their own houses. Also many of the prebendaries were appointed as incumbents of Abbey livings where, apart from their periods of residence and attendance at Chapter meetings, they often lived. I recall a Miss Mary Wordsworth, a great-niece of the poet who died on the eve of her hundredth birthday, telling me that when her father was a Canon of Westminster and also Rector of Stanford-in-the-Vale, only one house was kept furnished for the canons, the others being let.

The Dean, according to the Statutes, is the Governor of the whole College who shall be as 'the mind in the body'. To his authority all the others are to be obedient. As to the canons prebendaries) they both by their 'solemnity and prudence shall be even as chiefs and leaders in a Republic whom all the rest should honour and whose action the majority follow'.

The first Dean of the new Collegiate Church – there were three between the dissolution of the monastery and its revival by Mary – was William Bill who held office for only one year. His successor was Gabriel Goodman (1529?–1601), a scholar who translated the Epistle to the Corinthians for the Bishops' Bible and whose love for his native Wales manifested itself in the endowment of a hospital at Ruthven, his birthplace. He was an intimate friend of the great Elizabethan statesman, Lord Burghley. Goodman's solemn portrait adorns the gallery in the Deanery.

Times were difficult when Goodman took over. Chapter was like a house divided against itself and once again the Abbey was fortunate in having as Dean one who was as good by nature as he was by name. His tenure of office came at a significant period in history. Queen Elizabeth was engaged in a life-and-death struggle to maintain the integrity of the Church of England, threatened by various Protestant sects, products, in part, of the Continental Reformation. She wished for a liberal inclusive Church, loyal to the Throne and using the Book of Common Prayer. People could interpret its formularies as they pleased so long as they avoided public religious controversy. In this policy Gabriel Goodman was solidly behind her.

The two most talented Canons during his decanate were Lancelot Andrewes, whose *preces privatae* breathe a genuine piety and who was himself later appointed to the Deanery; and Richard Bancroft who left the Abbey to become Bishop of London prior to his elevation to Canterbury. He was largely responsible for an abortive codification of Canon Law which set out to regulate the lives of all Englishmen from the cradle to the grave.

Dean Goodman began with energy and determination to establish a church which managed its affairs 'decently and in order', seeking the support of Lord Burghley in so doing. He it was who drew up the Statutes which, as we have seen, he never persuaded the Queen to sign. He realized how important were the early years of the new church and that it was his responsibility to implement the Elizabethan Charter. He soon became aware of much slackness, for example in respect of the lay clerks who were in the habit of slipping out quietly during the sermon – a phenomenon not entirely unique to the sixteenth century. Such offenders were given a peremptory warning that henceforth they must be 'present at the service from the beginning to the end' and, if they were not, they would be fined 'for every default therein'! He was also aware of the shortcomings of some of his colleagues on the Chapter who failed to be present in the Choir 'to pray, as their most bounden duty was, for Her Majesty being their founder'. The trouble partly lay in a chronic shortage of prebendal houses, which encouraged both absenteeism and pluralism. However, Goodman was reluctant to push the prebendaries too far as he must largely depend on their cooperation. 'Hitherto', he wrote to Burghley, 'the company, thank God, have agreed very brotherly and with great quietness, as any company I hope: I would be sorry, if seeking to better things, division should grow.' Wise words! Burghley himself agreed, confessing that some of the prebendaries preferred to be 'left more at their liberty'.

The matter of prebendal houses long continued a problem, largely because of the destruction of older monastic property and the letting, on long leases, of most of the remaining houses in the precincts to laymen, often members of well-known families. A Chapter Minute of 31 January 1580/1 summarized the situation succinctly and suggested as a remedy 'that no lease shall hereafter be made of anie of the sayde late prebendaries houses until

such tymes that everye of the Prebendaries have solye to himself one house there to dwell in'. This was a solution but only a long-term one since obviously the existing leases could not be broken. The Dean and prebendaries were also forbidden, under heavy penalties, to lease any of their present houses to outsiders or any other buildings in the close except such as were obviously unsuitable for church purposes.

There was a little more to this Chapter Order than at first meets the eye. 'Further no Prebendary hereafter', so another minute runs, 'shall suffer anie woman beinge not his wife, mother, child or servante nor any other person to inhabbyte the said houses nor shall suffer any washinge or laundrye to be used in any of the said houses or any parte thereof.'

A major problem for a liberal dean like Goodman was the alarming infiltration of Puritans among the prebendaries. The effect of this was a 'non-conformity' which he found near unacceptable. 'Some', he wrote, 'come not in their habits, not to preach in the Church, because they have not subscribed unto the articles sent out unto us by my Lord of Canterbury in her Majesty's name.' During Goodman's period of office some forty prebendaries were installed, but many of them, in his view, were not highly talented. One who proved to be a menace was John Hardyman, a fanatical iconoclast who succeeded in 1561 in destroying a number of altars in the Abbey including that in the Confessor's Chapel when, according to the ecclesiastical historian, Strype, Queen Mary's 'diverse jewells' disappeared forever. Fortunately his misplaced zeal led to his being deprived of his office before the year was out.

Being at the Abbey for so long made it possible for Dean Goodman to 'try, try and try again'. Quite obviously the general approach and behaviour of the prebendaries was significant so far as the whole community was concerned. 'If gold rust what must iron do?' In 1586 he listed all the prebendaries by name, the preferments held by them, and which of them were married. Some indication as to the unsettlement of the times is

Educationalist and philanthropist Gabriel Goodman was as good by name as by nature. He completed forty years at the Abbey as Dean – a record, and desperately needed at the time to promote stability for the newly constituted Collegiate Church.

seen in an order which decreed that a member of the Chapter who possessed a key to the common garden could be fined up to ten shillings for any damage caused by him either deliberately or by negligence.

The general unrest sometimes spilled over and infected the servants, in which case they were given very short shrift. 'If anie servante', it was decreed, 'either of Mr Deane or of anie of the prebendaries ... or anie college servante shall by fighting, quarrelling or anie unseemlie manner so misbehave himself within the confines of the precincts, then, after due warning, he would be expelled. If, however, relying upon his own master's support, he should refuse to leave, he could be further fined £10, payable either to the Dean or to the prebendary directly involved in the dispute.' This decree was strictly enforced.

Most certainly Goodman was the right man to start the Collegiate Church of St Peter on its new

Sir Francis Vere, famous Elizabethan soldier. 'When his weapons he had cast aside, death like a coward struck him and he died.'

historic journey. The Abbey needed someone as responsible and vigilant as was Gilbert Crispin centuries earlier during an equally critical period. Goodman, to quote a contemporary, was a 'restorer rather than a devastator'. During his forty-year reign he set the new College on its feet and jealously guarded its rights and privileges. Thus he declined to allow the Canterbury convocation to meet at Westminster until he obtained an unequivocal declaration that 'no Archbishop or Bishop could exercise any ecclesiastical jurisdiction in it without leave of the Dean for the time being'. He pleaded before the House of Commons for the retention of the rights of sanctuary, and in spite of certain modifications was not unsuccessful.

Yet it was not always easy for Goodman to keep order within the Precincts and a measure of their disorder may be seen in a proclamation, fastened on the church doors, which he issued for the 'avoyding of brawles, frayes and quarrells in Church'. The background to all this was the increasing and fratricidal religious unsettlement.

However, we must not think of Gabriel Goodman only in these somewhat negative terms. He engaged himself actively in extensive repair work on the Abbey, particularly on the organ, and donated two bells which are still in use. His educational interest was life-long both in his Welsh benefactions and at Westminster where he endowed scholarships. In 1587 he re-equipped the College Library with shelving and desks. Four years later he rehoused it in what had been the old dormitory.

Gabriel Goodman was a great patron of William Camden, whom he appointed librarian, and defrayed the expenses of the research for his *Britannia,* a work written 'to awaken the interests of his countrymen to the history and beauty of the English countryside'. Goodman even wrote some Latin verses in praise of the author. He made his house a centre for many Welshmen of talent who came to London. In 1588 William Morgan while seeing his Welsh Bible through the press stayed at the Deanery, as also did Thomas Meredith who became Goodman's secretary.

One of his greatest gifts – he was a munificent benefactor to the Abbey – was the securing of Chiswick Manor for the Collegiate Church, which when the plague hit London enabled Westminster boys to continue their education in what was then the country. Lest we should be accused of painting too rosy a picture it needs to be said that, in the interests of the Abbey, Goodman was often extravagant and at least one prebendary, Dr Grant, accused him of wasting the College's substance. Certainly the Dean's 'borrowings' appear regularly in the Treasurer's account books.

A sensitive man, he took his responsibilities seriously and in the process earned the verdict of Archbishop Parker that he was a 'sad, grave man' but 'too severe'. The monument to Goodman in St Benedict's Chapel is one of the finest in the Abbey. Perhaps it is appropriate that he should be shown on his knees at prayer.

After the death of Goodman – his forty-year tenure of office is a record – there were six deans before the Collegiate Church was suppressed and its personnel dispersed at the time of the Commonwealth. The first of these was Lancelot Andrewes who, from the lofty heights of theological speculation and personal devotion, participated in the Coronation of James I, and presided over the memorialization of Mary, Queen of Scots. Less distinguished were his efforts to discipline fractious lay-vicars while his withdrawal to Chiswick House when London was visited with bubonic plague occasioned much criticism in the Precincts. It was Westminster School which commanded his greatest interest.

His successor was Richard Neile, a protégé of Goodman, a clumsy, sycophantic courtier, who though no scholar was a far better businessman than the learned Andrewes. He placed the altar at the east end of the church and did much repair work on the Abbey itself. He it was who secured a prebendal stall for William Laud.

His successor, George Montaigne, was the butt of many an apocryphal story. His father was reputed to be a small farmer and his mother a beggar woman from around Lincoln. He accompanied the second Earl of Essex on his expedition to Cadiz where he displayed 'such personal valour that, out of his gown, he would turn his back to no man'. A High Church man, he had more Laudian zeal than most and a contemporary describes him as 'one that loved his own ease too well to distort the concernments of the Church'. A man of inordinate ambition, he was not liked by the King but went off as Bishop of Lincoln (later to York) on the strength, so enemies facetiously maintained, of his suggesting to Charles: 'Hadst thou faith as a grain of mustard seed, thou wouldst say to this *mountain* be thou removed, and be thou cast into the *sea*.'

Robert Townson was in office for only three years before becoming Bishop of Salisbury, but during this time he had a memorable encounter with a great man in highly exceptional circumstances such as must have left an indelible impression upon him for the rest of his days. Sir Walter Raleigh, that intrepid old seafarer, was confined in the Gate House prison at the west end of the Abbey where Townson ministered to him on the eve of his execution.

The account which the Dean gave in a letter to Sir Justinian Isham, though it does him little credit, sheds light on the characters of both. When he began to encourage Raleigh against the fear of death he seemed 'to make so light of it' that the Dean wondered whether this were not due to a 'humour of vain glory or carelessness or contempt of death'. Raleigh asked the Dean how a man could die with 'cheerfulness and courage' unless he were assured of 'the love and favour of God unto him'. At this point the Dean withdrew and Lady Raleigh joined her husband until midnight. The Dean was back again early giving Sir Walter the Sacrament but was 'surprised and disgusted' to find him so 'very cheerful and merry'. Hence he warned him that 'the hand of God had found him out'; but Raleigh remained cheerful, eating a hearty breakfast and smoking his pipe. The Dean accompanied him to the scaffold and was forced to admit that he was 'the most fearless of death that ever was known and most reverent and confident'. His last words on the scaffold, doubtless carefully prepared, were epic: 'So the heart be right, it is no matter which way the head lies'.

The last effective Dean of Westminster, John Williams, before Oliver Cromwell took over during the Commonwealth period, was a truly remarkable man. He had great energy, talent and deep human sympathies, but was outrageously ambitious and took little pains to conceal it. He cultivated James I and the Duke of Buckingham assiduously, though this did not prevent him on occasions giving unpalatable advice. He had long cast his eye enviously in the direction of the Abbey, since *inter alia* it would provide him with a convenient lodging in London near to Whitehall. The list of his preferments before he went to Salisbury as Dean was legion, yet on 12 March 1620 he wrote to Buckingham suggesting that by

This magnificent Library (LEFT) was given by Dean Williams and is where his portrait hangs. It contains a collection of medieval monastic documents which defies comparison with any in Europe. 'A good book is the precious life-blood of a master spirit embalmed and treasured up on purpose for a life beyond life.'

The entry to 'Up School' which was once the monks' dormitory. The signatories have certainly left a name behind them.

his 'happy hand' he might be 'transplanted from Salisbury to Westminster'. Consequently he was installed in the Collegiate Church of St Peter as Dean on 12 July 1620 aged thirty-eight, holding this office for twenty-four years along with the bishopric of Lincoln and then the primacy of York – and this in spite of various efforts by Archbishop Laud and Charles I to get rid of him. He was amongst the most colourful Deans of Westminster and one of its most generous benefactors. He began by spending some £4,500 of his own money, in addition to what he found already in the Fabric Fund, on restoring the south-east end of the Abbey and the north-west front, adorning this with statues, including one of Abbot Islip whom he esteemed highly. He took a personal interest in Westminster School, and the scholars were often in the Deanery. Within the church he converted a room that was once the monks' dormitory into a 'goodly library' which, so comments his chaplain, Hacket, he 'model'd into a decent shape, furnished it with desks and chairs, accoutred it with all utensils, stored it with a vast number of learned volumes', to the value of some £2,000, and persuaded many of his wealthy friends to contribute on an equally generous scale. This Library, which is still in use, is one of the Abbey's greatest treasures. On one of its walls there hangs a full-length portrait of the Dean in which he appears in the traditional white ruff and wide-brimmed clerical hat. He is shown surveying his own creation with a sly, bland smile 'which must often have disconcerted enemies', of which he had not a few.

The Dean was a Welshman and proud of it. Not surprisingly, therefore, music was one of his great pleasures. He possessed a fine tenor voice and would frequently show it off by singing the service. He actively endeavoured to improve standards and to secure 'the sweetest music both for the organ and the voices of all parts that ever was heard in an English choir'. With a shrewd, practical common sense he realized that a powerful way of promoting this was to increase the salaries of the organist, the Choir and the Precentor. Also, through the Dean and Chapter, he provided accommodation for the singing men.

There was something almost attractive in the Dean's extravagance. On occasions everything had to be larger than life and perhaps the most spectacular of these was at the celebrations for Prince Charles' betrothal to Henrietta Maria of France. There was a magnificent party in Jerusalem Chamber. The afternoon began by the French Ambassador attending sung Evensong in the choir when he is reported to have gone to sleep during the service, and on being given a fine volume containing the Church of England Liturgy conveniently to have left it behind. The guests then moved into the Chamber for the reception. The Dean commemorated this event by erecting a fine wooden mantelpiece over the fireplace on which the heads of the Prince and Princess were delicately carved.

Although Williams could usually rely on the support of a majority of the Chapter there were on it two sworn enemies, Laud and Heylin, who often tried to rally the others against him. Indeed, the latter, a more exact scholar than Williams, though singularly bad-tempered, went so far as to maintain a vendetta against him, working hand in glove with Laud, a future Archbishop of Canterbury whose biography he wrote. It needs to be remembered that this conflict, though often petty and personal, was a reflection of religious and political divisions within the country. The nation was being increasingly fragmented and it was not easy for such as Williams who endeavoured to follow a middle way.

Williams became intimate with James I and offered him advice on the vexed question of monopolies. In 1621 when Francis Bacon was deprived of the high office of Lord Keeper of the Seal on his being condemned for taking bribes, Williams was nominated as his successor. In many respects this was a remarkable appointment, since the Dean was a clergyman and no lawyer. In fact, he was the last ecclesiastic ever to hold so elevated a secular office. In political affairs, alas, the Dean often thought that the end justified the means. Thus when to obtain certain information he secured it from the Spanish ambassador's mistress, a spy, he justified himself in these words: 'I have gleaned up this maxim: it is lawful to make use of the sin of another. Though the devil made her a sinner, I may make good use of her sin.'

Ever since 1628 a Star Chamber prosecution had been in process against Williams for an alleged breach of confidentiality in betraying secrets known to him as a privy councillor. (This has a peculiarly contemporary ring about it.) He now added to his indiscretions by suborning false evidence in favour of a man whose testimony he

Francis Holles died at the age of eighteen, having served through the Flemish campaign. A bereaved father, in extreme grief, erected this memorial. He is dressed as a Roman soldier.

was anxious to secure. In 1633 he was again brought before the Star Chamber on this additional charge and on 11 July 1637 was fined £10,000 to go to the King and 10,000 marks to Sir John Morrison whom he had also wronged. In addition to the fines he was deprived of the income from all his benefices, sentenced to be imprisoned during His Majesty's pleasure, and the exercise of his various offices to be suspended. Further charges were brought against him which related to

documents found in his episcopal house at Buckden in which Laud was described as 'the little urchin' and the 'meddling hocus-pocus'. After some three years in the Tower of London he was unconditionally released in 1640.

Williams' resilience and ability to come back were extraordinary. The Puritans were now agitating for the abolition of episcopacy, to offset which Williams introduced a bill into Parliament for the 'regulation of bishops'. They must be required to preach regularly and should be helped in exercising their jurisdiction and pastoral ministry by assistant bishops. As for appointments to the episcopate, the bishops should send three names to the King from which he would choose one.

Charles, as things grew increasingly serious, certainly endeavoured to win the support of more moderate opinion by appointing bishops whose ability and character would give confidence to responsible people. As a consequence the almost impossible happened with the nomination of Williams, on 8 December 1641, to the Archbishopric of York. His troubles, however, were not yet over. On going to the House of Lords on 27 December he and his fellow bishops, so great was Puritan hostility against them, were molested and could not enter Parliament.

The bishops collectively petitioned against this affront, protesting that as they could not safely attend the House all the laws, orders and votes recorded in their absence were null and void. For this display of independence they were impeached by the Commons, and twelve bishops, including Williams, were sent off to the Tower, a by now familiar habitat. Soon Williams was released on bail, which he broke by going to York for his enthronement as Archbishop on 27 June 1642, an office which he titularly held until 1650. On the outbreak of the Civil War he retired to Conway in Wales and was put forward by his countrymen as their leader after the disastrous royalist defeat at Naseby. In 1648 his realism and practical cast of mind manifested themselves in his making terms with the parliamentary commander Thomas Mytton.

Here we must leave Archbishop Williams. If his policy was ultimately right, all too often his methods were wrong. However, Westminster Abbey is greatly indebted to him for the generosity of his benefactions.

When an eminent ecclesiastic was once apprised

of the death of a distinguished headmaster he remained for a moment in deep thought, then said quietly: 'This persuades me more than ever that there must be an intermediate state.' Perhaps this could equally be said of John Williams, sometime Dean of Salisbury, Dean of Westminster, Bishop of Lincoln and Archbishop of York.

The flight of Dean Williams to the North, never to return to Westminster, and the triumph of the Parliamentary forces led to an astonishing era in the life (or non-life) of the Abbey after a century of bewildering change. A Puritan takeover followed the last meeting of the Dean and Chapter, held on 25 May 1642 when the minutes were signed by Robert Newell, Peter Heylin, and five other prebendaries. There was a mass exodus from the Precincts, as the Collegiate Church of St Peter was suppressed by law. A committee of twenty members of Parliament, followed by a board of gover-

This fine mantlepiece (LEFT) was placed in Jerusalem Chamber by Dean Williams to commemorate the reception there in connection with the betrothal of Prince Charles to Henrietta Maria of France.

nors, was set up to run the Abbey which became a Puritan preserve and preaching-shop. However the finances were never more carefully handled than by these eminent men. They did much to repair the fabric of the Church and, *mirabile dictu*, the Royal tombs; also to increase the revenues from the estates. So the Commonwealth was established, but directing the overall affairs of the State presented severe problems. Oliver Cromwell was impaled on the horns of a dilemma. He believed in a democratic system, yet at the same time in the rule of the Saints, although the two are incompatible. With the death of the Great Protector, there passed with him into history the memory of a noble, if wishful dream. Nostalgia for a known way, the inquisitorial entry of the Puritans into so many areas of private and domestic life and the romantic aura of the young King 'over the water' led to the restoration of monarchy in 1660, and Charles II's splendid and euphoric Coronation. It is to coronations in the Abbey that we now turn.

Ceiling boss in the Muniment Room, depicting a combat between a man and a lion centaur.

EIGHT

Coronations

Often when I have given a lecture on coronations I have been asked: 'Is it a great state occasion or is it a religious service?' My reply is always the same, 'Why can't it be both?' The answer is that it can. The whole intention of the ceremony is to bridge the divide between God and his world; the sacred and the secular; the kingdom of God and the kingdoms of men. The Abbey, because of its distinctive past, is admirably suited and historically conditioned to be a church in which coronations take place.

The Coronation Service goes back to the distant days of the early Teutons when the ruler, on his elevation, was hoisted on a shield by the chiefs of the tribe. Later the Church added its distinctive theological framework to this ancient custom, thus giving it a religious character. This did not mean, however, that it ceased to be political. Indeed the sacred and the secular in those early days were one and indivisible. In Anglo-Saxon England the Order of the Rite, probably an adaptation of that used for Frankish imperial coronations, can be traced back to King Edgar, who, having succeeded to the throne at the age of sixteen in AD 957, was crowned some twenty years later at Bath on Whit Sunday in the presence of a vast assembly of the Witan. This is the first Coronation of which a full description has survived and the first occasion on which, it would seem, the Archbishops of Canterbury and Northumbria took part in the crowning of an English king. This basic form has survived, with modifications, to this day.

King Edgar entered the church wearing his crown and laid it before the altar. Dunstan, Archbishop of Canterbury, then began the *Te Deum*. At its conclusion the bishops raised the King from his knees, and at Dunstan's dictation he then took a three-fold oath that he would ensure that the Church of God and all Christian people

The Abbey ready and laid out for a coronation in the seventeenth century.

enjoyed true peace for ever; that he would forgive all wrong and robbery to all degrees; and would command justice and mercy in all judgements. Then the consecration prayers were said upon which the Archbishop anointed Edgar, the antiphon 'Zadok the priest' being sung and all joining in the shout 'Let the King live for ever'. Dunstan next invested the King with the ring and sword, placed the crown on his head and the sceptre and rod in his hands. Both Archbishops enthroned him. The whole ceremony was framed within the Mass and thus wedded to the deepest insights of Christian faith and piety.

The problem for monarchs, representing as they did the unity of the nation, was to ensure that potential pockets of resistance should not be allowed to fester into open rebellion. Safely ensconced in his walled castle in pre-gunpowder days, the medieval baron could be almost impregnable. The coronation, through a most solemn oath of fealty, bound him to his liege lord. On the other hand, the King is pledged to see himself as under God's final sovereignty and accountable to him. Thus he is bound to respect the 'liberties' and the legitimate rights of the subjects over whom he reigns.

There is an early tradition that Harold the Saxon was crowned in St Edward's Abbey church but the evidence for this is doubtful. What *is* certain is that on Christmas Day 1066 there strode into the brand new Abbey church, not yet complete, William, Duke of Normandy. He claimed to be the legitimate successor of the saintly Edward whose body lay before the high altar; he held a papal brief to bring England back into the bosom of the Catholic Church from which it had been severed by the schismatic Stigand, Archbishop of Canterbury. William, moreover, had validated his claims by victory in the field. But he was not content. He must follow the precedents set by former Anglo-Saxon monarchs and be crowned, thus adding to his other claims a divine sanction, and binding his subjects to him by solemn oaths.

William's Coronation in the Abbey was indeed an extraordinary affair since he was being crowned in a hostile city and Norman guards were posted around the church. When at the time of the Recognition the customary question was put to the congregation in English and in French, receiving a vociferous assent, the guards mistakenly assumed that there was a rebellion within the church and consequently charged in. To add to the general confusion some outhouses were set on fire and the smoke drifted into the Abbey. Not surprisingly, the congregation panicked and rushed out, leaving only the Conqueror and the officiating clergy. So 'in the solitude of that wintry day, amidst the cries of his new subjects, trampled down by the horses' hoofs of their conquerors, he himself for the first time in his life trembled from head to foot, as the remainder of the service was hurried on'. He could not have known, even have suspected, that over a period of some nine hundred years every monarch of England, with the two exceptions of Edward v and Edward viii, would be crowned and anointed in Westminster Abbey. This succession is now unique in Western Europe.

However, comments Dr L. E. Tanner, a former Librarian and Keeper of the Muniments, Westminster Abbey still lacked something truly symbolic which could encapsulate the 'heart of the matter' like the famous St Augustine's chair at Canterbury. It was left to Edward I to provide what was needed when he brought back to Westminster the Stone of Scone taken from the Scots in 1296. Many have speculated on the precise origins and history of the stone though there is no lack of romantic stories to fill in the gaps where history is silent. Even Jacob at Bethel has been mentioned in this context. Geologists assert that it dates back to the Lower Old Red Sandstone Age of which there is much in the neighbourhood of Scone. The stone has been taken as signifying kingly rule and as such Edward placed it in St Edward's Chapel. His first intention was to insert the stone in a bronze chair, but this, for one reason or another, possibly expense, was abandoned for a painted wooden one. Though restored, it remains in a somewhat mutilated condition. Carved inscriptions on the back and the seat of the chair inform us that at least one Westminster schoolboy slept in the chair overnight. It was used at Edward II's coronation – the first held in the new church and equally the first occasion when a Queen (Eleanor) was crowned with her husband.

The stone has left the Abbey on three occasions, once when taken over to Westminster Hall for the installation of Oliver Cromwell as Lord Protector; the second when it was taken to Gloucester during World War II; and the third when it was removed from the Abbey by two young Scottish students on Christmas Eve 1950 and taken back to Scotland. Folklore around this event is already growing. It is said that a highly disturbed Dean, Alan Don, a Scotsman from Dundee, rushed round to Archdeacon Fox in Little Cloister and, finding him in bed, roused him gasping out the words, 'Adam, the stone has been stolen,' to which the unruffled Archdeacon replied: 'I'm glad to hear it.' The stone was found some three months later deposited before the erstwhile High Altar at Arbroath. I can recall seeing an anxious clerk of works, Harry Bishop, another Scotsman, on the eve of his going up to Arbroath to identify the stone and bring it safely back to the Abbey.

As the years went on, the coronation tended to grow by the accretion of new elements. Thus at Richard II's in 1377, there was introduced for the first time the procession from the Tower to Westminster; also there appeared a body of young men as Knights of the Bath.

It was at Henry IV's Coronation that the office of King's Champion was finally confirmed in favour of the Dymoke family, a great victory for the redoubtable Dame Margery of Ludlow, a militant lady who boasted of her determination 'not to take off her slippers while she went to bed' until justice had been done.

The death of Henry IV has been given a dramatic interest through Shakespeare's *Henry IV, Part 2*. What is certain in respect of this event is that Prince Henry ('Hal') spent the night of his father's death at the Abbey and so tradition asserts, passed some time with the anchorite. His Coronation is the only one which has a contemporary reproduction in the church, which may be seen on the side of his Chantry Chapel.

With the advent of the Reformation and England's separation from Rome, coronations were bound to be affected; and as a result Tudor coronations, subsequent to Henry VII and Henry VIII, had certain curious ingredients. At the enthroning of Edward VI, the boy king, on 20 February 1547, Archbishop Cranmer used three crowns, St Edward's, the Imperial Crown and 'a very new one' specially made for the occasion. The two following days were given over to jousting witnessed by the child monarch. Queen Mary's Coronation reverted to type, but with the coming of her half-sister Elizabeth it was recognized that certain changes must be made. At this ceremony, which took place on 15 January 1559, Mass was sung as of old but the Gospel was read in English as well as in Latin. It was, though minimal, a significant compromise typical of Elizabeth's cautious temperament.

But who was to conduct this ceremony? Canterbury was vacant through the death of Cardinal Pole; the Archbishop of York declined; Tunstall of Durham was too old. Hence this duty fell to Owen Oglethorpe of Carlisle, who discharged it with reluctance. Indeed, his subsequent agonizing scruples for what he had done were said to have

The beautiful Eleanor of Castile, wife of Edward I. Accompanying the King on a crusade, she protested: 'The way to Heaven is as near from Palestine as from England'.

hastened his death. The bishops were present in force, except Bonner of London, who, however, lent his robes for the occasion.

Charles I's Coronation, so many recalled in the light of subsequent tragic events, was full of forebodings and impending doom. At the Recognition there was an ominous silence and the congregation had to be instructed to give voice with 'God save the King'. The text chosen for the sermon seemed to presage Charles's grim end on a scaffold: 'Be thou faithful unto death, and I will give thee a crown of life.'

Oliver Cromwell, for religious reasons, preferred to hold his 'installation' – this designation was carefully chosen – as Lord Protector, not in the Abbey but in Westminster Hall to where the coronation chair was moved.

Charles II began his reign, according to his royalist supporters and constitutional historians, at the precise moment of his father's death. During the Commonwealth he wandered about Europe, advised for a time by a Dean of Westminster,

Richard Steward, who was never destined to enter into office. Charles's triumphant return to England on 25 May 1660 was greeted with ecstatic enthusiasm and, by some, with a nauseating fanaticism. The bodies of Oliver Cromwell and the regicides buried in Henry VII's Chapel were dug up and hanged on a gibbet, and their heads were impaled on spikes on Westminster Hall. It is but fair to Charles II, probably agnostic in religion, to say that such dreadful obscenities gave him no pleasure. He did not share the persecuting spirit of those who wished to wreak vengeance but prudently did not actively oppose them.

Some time ago, when Alan Don was Dean of Westminster, he received a request from its owner to re-inter the head of Oliver Cromwell in the Abbey where his corpse had originally been buried. The Dean, after careful enquiry, felt satisfied that this really was the head of the Lord Protector but was of opinion that he must decline this request. Had I been Dean then, my wish would have been to say 'yes', though its implementation would have needed the approval of the Visitor.

As to Charles II's Coronation, those in charge of its planning felt that everything must be done to stress continuity with the past. Hence it should be splendid and magnificent, a truly great occasion. Politically the assumption was that the Commonwealth had never been. England had now returned to the good old days under a heroic prince who had endured untold suffering before he had entered into his rightful inheritance. Prebendary Heylin, preaching in the Abbey after the Coronation on the anniversary of the King's return, strained his considerable resources of language to draw a comparison between Charles and King David, greatly to the detriment of the latter. 'To his people', he said, 'whose tears he put into his bottle; whose stripes he bore in his own body, and whose calamities did more to afflict his righteous Soul than his own misfortune, he now came as a Prince of Peace, as the Son of David, to bring the glad tidings of Salvation to all his subjects, to put an end to all the miseries of his people and to restore to

Supporting column on the tomb of Ludovic, Duke of Richmond and Lennox. This is an enormous monument with bronze symbolic figures of hope, truth, charity and faith holding up a canopy. Many Stuarts lie buried nearby, including Esmé, Duke of Richmond and Lennox.

them that peace and happiness, which they have forfeited by pride and weakness, by disobedience to his Person.' It is a pity that Charles II was not in the Abbey when this sermon was delivered. It would have given him a great deal of amusement as he wondered who on earth the preacher was talking about.

But to return to Charles's Coronation. It will occasion no surprise that the inimitable Samuel Pepys managed to gain access to the Abbey for this great event, arriving there at 4.30 a.m., and possibly doing a bit of gate crashing. The colour and the pageantry excited him; the sight of the King 'bare-headed', was 'very fine'. Alas, he could not catch any of the silver medals flung up and down by Lord Cornwallis and was unable to hear much of the music because of the din.

James II's Coronation on St George's Day 1685 is among the best-documented but was, of course, somewhat truncated since he was a Roman Catholic and therefore could not receive the Sacrament. Thus the service of Holy Communion was entirely omitted, but he submitted to being crowned by the Primate of All England.

The events of James II's reign cannot be dealt with here. They are magnificently, though one-sidedly, told by Lord Macaulay. Who could better his reflections on the birth of the Young Pretender, destined to receive 'flattery more galling than insults and hopes such as make the heart grow sick'? Suffice it to say that this perverse monarch rashly pursued two incompatible policies at the same time – to increase the power of the Crown and to advance the Roman Catholic cause. His reign consequently lasted only three years, by which time events had moved on to a crisis.

At least the King had one sympathizer, if not active supporter, at the Abbey in the person of Thomas Sprat, the Dean. He read James II's 'Declaration on the Liberty of Conscience in the Collegiate Church', though many parishes declined to do so, but there was 'so great a murmur and noise that nobody could hear'. A Westminster schoolboy recalled that few prebendaries were in their stalls with the choir-boys and King's scholars but that Sprat could hardly hold the Proclamation in his hand for trembling.

Also when on the acquittal of the Seven Bishops the bells were rung in jubilation from many a London tower, including the Abbey, Dean Sprat gave peremptory orders that this must cease forth-

with. (Thomas Sprat has at least one claim to remembrance as the historian of the Royal Society!)

In 1689 for the first time in a long history, and so far not repeated, William of Orange and Mary, daughter of James II by his first wife Anne Hyde, and fully regnant, were both offered the Crown, on their joint or single lives. Their two heads, until Mary's death, appeared on the coinage of the realm and another chair was made for the new Queen at her enthroning. The Coronation, held on 11 April 1689, gave validity and added force to the Whig theory of a 'compact' between sovereign and subjects which, if seriously contravened, could be brought to an end. William, though a grandson of Charles I by his daughter Mary, had no claim to the throne on the grounds of 'legitimacy'. Indeed if it be allowed that James's flight was in effect an abdication, and that the story of the warming pan and the birth of the Old Pretender was fact and not fiction, this would still remain true.

The taking of oaths to the new Government presented a serious problem to many conscientious High Anglicans. Archbishop Sancroft felt that he just could not repeat the same oaths to another and as a consequence joined the ranks of the Non-Jurors. Dean Sprat was not happy with the situation, but in spite of his High Church Toryism and theoretical devotion to Filmer's doctrine of the 'Divine Right of Kings', he in the end subscribed. As to why he had done this Sancroft rather unkindly said to him: 'My dear Brother, I will tell you the reason; you cannot live on forty pounds a year as I can.' If this had been the case then perhaps remarks about him by the Earl of Aylesbury were relevant: 'He was a man of worth, but loved hospitality beyond his purse.'

The Bishop of London, Henry Compton, who presided at William and Mary's coronation in the absence of Sancroft, gained some notoriety by declaring that he could not think of any oaths to the Government that he would not be prepared to take. He was no academic liturgiologist but a practical man who introduced into the coronation rite something which struck a chord in most breasts – the presentation of the Bible to the sovereign as 'the most valuable thing that this world affords. Here is wisdom: This is the Royal Law: These are the lively Oracles of God.'

As to how far the twelve prebendaries of the Abbey entertained scruples of conscience about taking the oaths we cannot tell. If they had, they certainly overcame them, for without exception they conformed.

One who might have been thought to entertain difficulties in recognizing the new monarch was Francis Atterbury, who became Dean of Westminster in 1713, but this does not appear to have been the case at the time. Atterbury was as brilliant as he was handsome, nor could one deny the magnetism of his personality. He was an extremely high churchman, affectionate in friendship, but wherever he went, whether it were Christchurch, Carlisle or Westminster, he became engaged in emotional conflicts with his colleagues. He was received warmly on his coming – South, a prebendary, was at Westminster School with him – but the usual pattern of strife and division was not long in making itself felt. The story of these days is rich in human interest but, alas, we must pass it by. More serious in respect of his tenure of office as Dean and as Bishop of Rochester was his Jacobitism which at first was romantic and nostalgic rather than treasonable and dangerously political. In a pamphlet he pleaded for clemency for the rebels after the abortive rebellion in 1715 and was said to have been prepared to proclaim James III at Charing Cross. 'Never was a better cause lost for want of spirit,' he maintained. His downfall came when he undoubtedly corresponded with the Old Pretender and was involved in a plan for invasion in 1722. A bill was passed through Parliament to exile him in spite of his brilliant but somewhat disingenuous defence. In exile he always retained the affection of many boys at Westminster School, and one who went with a group to see him in the Tower not long before he left England remembered his quoting Milton:

> The world was all before them, where to choose
> Their place of rest, and Providence their guide.

He lived nearly ten years in exile, remaining avid for Westminster news and dying in Paris on 4 March 1732. He was interred in a family vault in the Abbey where his wife's body lay, 'at the west door . . . as far from Kings and Kaisers as the space will admit of'.

What is significant about Atterbury's Jacobitism is that this was the last occasion on which a clergyman at the Abbey became so immediately and critically involved in national politics. The deans after him were depoliticized.

The next Coronation was that of Anne, Queen Mary's sister, which took place in the Abbey on 23 April 1702. One who was present describes it as a 'splendid occasion' though this does not tell us much about it! Significantly she passed over the Whig Archbishop Tenison and chose the Tory Archbishop of York, Sharpe, to give the address. On 1 August 1714 Queen Anne died, evoking the comment from Dr Arbuthnot, whom Swift describes as her 'favourite physician': 'Sleep was never more welcome to a weary traveller than death was to her.'

The next in succession under the Act of 1701 was the Electress Sophia of Hanover, a granddaughter of James I. It is curious to reflect that had Anne died some few weeks earlier she would have been crowned Queen of the United Kingdom. As it was, her son, the Elector of Hanover, ascended the throne as George I. The Coronation was held on 20 October 1714, 'with great pomp, both spiritual and lay peers of nearly every political complexion appearing in their places'. It was a day which the aged, gout-ridden, infirm Archbishop Tenison could only regard as providential, and he was determined to preside over it. This he did 'with a peculiar joy' in spite of 'great pain and difficulty', since he had long worked for, and had set great hopes upon, the Hanoverian succession.

The attitude towards, and the conduct of, coronations seem to constitute a kind of spiritual barometer in relation to the state of the nation. In the eighteenth century they in no sense suggested great religious occasions; indeed they were at 'an all-time low', being conducted in a most slovenly way. Horace Walpole found it difficult to take them seriously. It was not unusual when the preacher ascended the pulpit for members of the aristocracy to bring out their luncheon baskets, thus fortifying themselves against the ordeal ahead.

This does not mean that a great deal of money was not expended on coronations: rather that little attempt was made to inculcate a genuine atmosphere of prayer and dedication. An exception was the Coronation of George III, who on his accession boasted that 'born and educated in this country I glory in the name of Briton'. He was himself 'sincerely pious, his morality strict and he invariably acted according to the dictates, erroneous or otherwise, of his conscience'. He took his crowning seriously, but this cannot be said of his son George IV, whose undoubted flair for the arts was perhaps his one redeeming characteristic. With great natural talents, amusing and a facile wit, he has not unfairly been described as 'a bad son, a bad husband, a bad monarch and a bad friend'. His Coronation, in its great pomp, enormous expense, and complete exclusion of the public, was such as only to enhance his unpopularity. The royal robes alone cost £24,000 and the crown £54,000. The weather was hot and he mopped up oceans of perspiration with a succession of handkerchiefs during the ceremony. Also Queen Caroline tried desperately but in vain to gain entry. Popular support for the Queen derived more from dislike of George IV than from genuine affection for Caroline.

George IV's successor, William IV, the 'Sailor King', was indeed a different kind of animal, and remained to the end of his life a 'garrulous, homely, kind-hearted old man, fond of making speeches which were generally uncalled for, and frequently absurd; fierce in his dislikes but not vindictive, and liable to wild bursts of passion'. His instant response to his Coronation was to suggest that its expense was excessive; that it was unnecessary; and he had to be persuaded into it. The dignity and spiritual intention of the rite passed him by. Thus when that most moving moment was reached when he was ceremonially stripped of the emblems of the panoply of power there he stood, not in a simple white tunicle but splendiferous in the dress-uniform of an admiral of the fleet.

One practical problem, however, was overcome with commendable ingenuity. The singing of the Litany, with its versicles and responses, is not easily performed in so large a building when those participating are separated the one from the other by a considerable distance. The answer to this knotty problem, however, proved to be simple. A man with a green flag was placed in a strategic position between the participants with the responsibility of waving vigorously to give the 'all clear'. Apparently all went well!

Lord Macaulay was not, on the whole, impressed with the occasion, though attracted to its colour and pageantry. His letter describing it to his sister bears at least partial quotation:

The whole Abbey was one blaze of gorgeous dresses, mingled with lovely faces. The Queen behaved admir-

The coronation chair was constructed on the orders of Edward I to house the stone of Scone. 'This royal throne of kings, this sceptr'd isle, this earth of majesty, this seat of Mars.'

ably, with wonderful grace and dignity. The King very awkwardly. The Duke of Devonshire looked as if he came to be crowned instead of his master. I never saw so princely a manner and air. The Chancellor looked like Mephistopheles behind Margaret in the Church. The ceremony was much too long and some parts of it were carelessly performed. The Archbishop mumbled. The

Bishop of London preached well enough, indeed, but not so effectively as the occasion required; and above all the foolish parts of the ritual appeared monstrously ridiculous and deprived many of the better parts of their proper effect. Persons who were at a distance did not perhaps feel this, but I was near enough to see every turn of his [the King's] finger, and every glance of his eye. The moment of the crowning was extremely fine ... all the Peers and Peeresses put on their coronets, and the blaze of splendour through the Abbey seemed to be doubled.

This tells us a great deal about Lord Macaulay as well as the event he describes.

Coronations began to rediscover something of their real significance and solemnity with that of Queen Victoria who was crowned on 28 June 1838, and this in spite of the fact that at one level many things went wrong. She herself was just nineteen years of age, enthusiastic, accomplished and appealingly childlike. So great was public interest in her Coronation that it was estimated some 400,000 people came up to London to witness it, many bivouacking in the streets the night before. Queen Victoria tells us in her 'Diary' that she awoke early on what was to be a wonderful summer's day full of sunshine. The royal procession to the Abbey was revived for the first time since the Coronation of George III and the Queen left Buckingham Palace at 10 a.m., arriving at an Abbey elaborately decorated in crimson and gold. Dean Stanley, then a schoolboy, long remembered that as she entered 'with eight ladies all in white, floating about her like a silvery cloud; she paused, as if for breath, and clasped her hands. A ray of sunshine fell on her head as she knelt to receive the crown and the Duchess of Kent, her mother, burst into tears.' She had ceased to be a child. Alas, the ritual hardly went forward decently and in order. Lord Melbourne had warned her in advance that the two supporting bishops who stood on either side of her would not prove helpful – and he was right! 'Pray, tell me what I am to do, for they [the clergy] don't know', she exclaimed pathetically at one solemn moment to a lay official standing near her. She found the orb too heavy to hold and when the ruby ring was forced by the Archbishop on the wrong finger which began to swell she had to retire to St Edward's Chapel to remove it with a liberal application of soap and water. Lord Rolle, an eighty-year-old peer, in paying his homage, tripped as he was getting up the steps to the throne.

Before he could attempt another ascent the Queen herself advanced towards him 'an act of graciousness and kindness which made a great sensation'. The service seemingly at last ended – it took four hours – they retired into St Edward's Chapel only to find that the Archbishop had inadvertently turned over two pages in his script. The young Queen insisted that they return to the Sacrarium to complete the ceremony. The Dean of Westminster commented afterwards that there 'certainly ought to have been a rehearsal'. Perhaps he should have suggested one!

In spite of all these mishaps, the Queen's simplicity, her obvious dedication and her sincere concern to live out the responsibilities which the liturgy enshrined, redeemed the situation and made the occasion in the best sense memorable. Eighteenth-century rationalism and apathy were replaced by relevance and a touch of mystery. Carlyle, who was amongst the crowd and saw the Queen return 'pale and tremulous' to the Palace, 'breathed a blessing on her'. 'Poor little Queen,' he commented, 'she is at an age when a girl can hardly be trusted to choose a bonnet for herself; yet a task is laid upon her from which an archangel might shrink.' There was more steel in Victoria than he could have suspected at the time. Yet it is true that the first thing she did on returning to the Palace was to 'doff her splendours' in order to give her pet spaniel, Dash, its afternoon bath.

Westminster Abbey, it must be confessed, saw little of Queen Victoria across the years, certainly not in the congregation. Her marriage was conducted privately at St George's Chapel, Windsor, though she came to the Collegiate Church for her Golden Jubilee. Indeed she would probably have felt it indecent for her subjects to gaze upon her while at prayer – not, we hope, for the reason which prompted Dr Busby to ask Charles I, who was visiting Westminster School, for permission to keep his hat on in the royal presence since it would be bad for discipline if the scholars saw him paying deference to an earthly superior. However, the Queen had a link with the Abbey through her intimate friendship with Lady Augusta Stanley, wife of the Dean. They corresponded regularly and the Queen came to the Deanery, sometimes to learned scientific discussions. She visited Lady Augusta during her last illness in the Islip wing of the Deanery. Many of the Queen's letters, deeply edged in black after the death of the Prince

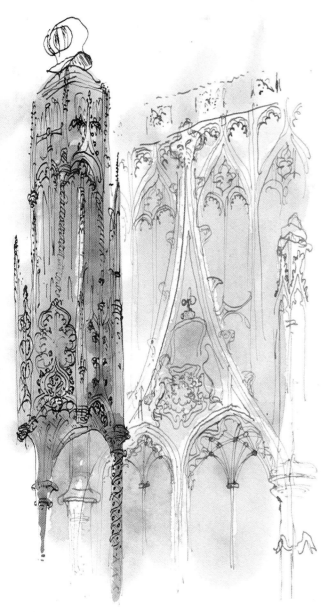

The glories of Henry VII Chapel have not been dulled or petrified by the passage of time.

Consort, are among the Abbey muniments in the Library. I remember when reading them having my curiosity aroused by the Queen's oft-repeated question: 'Has the Dean yet seen the Prince of Wales?' Lady Augusta's replies were usually prevaricating and evasive. Why the delay, I wondered? Finally, as I turned the pages, I found out. The Queen had asked the Dean to chide the Prince on his slackness in attending divine worship on Sundays. It is difficult to imagine any more uncongenial task for so liberal and eirenical a Dean.

Since Queen Victoria's there have been four coronations in the Abbey, all of which have shown an increasing recognition of their seriousness, significance and potential spirituality.

The Coronation of Edward VII had to be postponed from its original date of 26 June 1902 to 9 August because of an operation for peritonitis from which he made a good recovery, though some had even doubted his survival. It was an impressive occasion and the King entered into the spirit of it solemnly and sincerely. The aged Archbishop Temple, a rugged and dedicated Christian, struggled through in spite of the handicap of very poor sight. There still remains in the Abbey Library his chaplain's hand-written lettering of enormous size which he held up before the Archbishop page by page as he laboured on with the service. The crowning, alas, was marred by the Archbishop in his near blindness putting the crown on the King's head the wrong way round so that it was necessary to remove it and put it on again. It was a pity that the lights in the Abbey were not switched on earlier so some complained. Sir William St John Hope, an eminent antiquary, was critical of matters concerning which most members of the congregation would have cared little. He saw no sign of any putting on of the *Colobium Sindonis*, nor did the Duke of Newcastle present the glove. The crown with which the King was crowned was not that of St Edward as directed by the Coronation Order but the Imperial Crown. The Bishop of Durham gave incorrect whispered directions to the King and Queen after the consecration in the communion service which he had to contradict to the total confusion of those present. The same critic condemned the 'contemptible sham antique structure set up at the western end of the church' – i.e. the annexe. It is clear that the rehearsals for this Coronation were inadequate, though perhaps nothing could have overcome the difficulties sight-wise with which the aged Archbishop had to cope.

Fortunately these shortcomings were progressively overcome through more meticulous preparation and the clear recognition that so intricate a ceremony could not be grasped by the light of nature alone but needed rehearsals for everyone concerned as in a theatrical performance.

Much of course depended on the Archbishop as the second most important person in the coronation ceremony. Randall Davidson presided over the Coronation of George v on 22 June 1911. Both he and the King were unostentatious and though Davidson was better educated and more subtle in his approach, both had great integrity and were modest and unaffected. The Coronation itself bore the imprint of restraint. It fell to Davidson to deal with Asquith in connection with the monarch's declaration with its offensive reference to Roman Catholics. It was, given the Protestant feeling of the day, a difficult problem and Davidson was unsuccessful in getting the changes he either desired or was prepared to accept.

It would be difficult to find two persons, both Scotsmen, more different in temperament or attitude than Randall Davidson and Cosmo Lang his successor at Lambeth. The latter was a dramatic character with a splendidly rich and sonorous voice which responded to his various moods and many-sided temperament. He had a great sense of theatre – his brother was Matheson Lang, the actor – and he was always tempted to dramatize human situations.

It was particularly important, in view of Edward VIII's abdication, that George VI's Coronation in 1937 should in no sense suggest an anti-climax. As much as in 1660 a supreme effort was needed to give this ceremony contemporary relevance and to give full publicity to a shy king who did not seek this high office and who had not the gifts of his more extrovert brother. But George VI had two great assets: humility with a tremendous dedication to doing his best for the nation in totally unexpected circumstances, and his wife Queen Elizabeth. A wave of sympathy and encouragement supported the couple, and the Coronation – in spite of appalling weather – caught up this mood and thus in its own way was distinguished.

Two new features were introduced into this ceremony: a restrained use of the radio and the recording of a film. Both served to make the occasion real to thousands who were not in the Abbey or thronging the streets.

George VI's last appearance in public was at an installation of the Order of the Bath in Henry VII's Chapel in 1951. Much to the surprise of the Dean, he asked that his sword should be laid on the altar during the somewhat elaborate ceremonial. The Dean pointed out that this had never been done before and thus formed no part of the traditional rite. However, the King properly had his way and this was done. On 6 February 1952 he died while his daughter Elizabeth and her husband Philip, Duke of Edinburgh, were away on a state visit in Kenya. They returned immediately, in time for the interment of the King's mortal remains at St George's Chapel, Windsor, and the ritual pattern which preceded it.

When this was completed the traditional procedure to organize a coronation was set in hand. The Earl Marshal, the Duke of Norfolk, took over and to him Abbey personnel handed their keys. This meant that sung services, weekdays and Sundays, ceased, the offices being said in St Faith's Chapel. Apart from the canon in residence and a minor canon who stayed put, the clergy accepted invitations to give addresses on the coronation and to preach all over the country. In the Abbey a vast transformation took place giving an extended theatre under the Sacrarium and providing three tiers, thus making it possible to house a congregation of some eight thousand people.

In between the previous coronation and that of 1953 there had been a grim World War. The national mood had now changed; the Empire had given place, or was in process of doing so, to a Commonwealth of autonomous, self-governing states. The Archbishop of Canterbury, Dr Geoffrey Fisher, was responsible to the Earl Marshal for the due performance of the ancient rite and for any changes made in it. To help him in the discharge of this duty he nominated a small committee consisting in the main of liturgical scholars; as also did the Director of Music to which post Dr William McKie, organist and Master of the Choristers of the Abbey, was appointed.

There were three areas in relation to the ceremony which were of concern: whether the age-old, feudal and traditional rite would still register and commend itself as relevant in 1953; whether the moderator of the general assembly of representatives of the Church of Scotland, and the Commonwealth ought to be brought into the ceremony and if so how; and whether the full resources of broadcasting, in particular television, should be deployed.

As to the first, there were not a few people who felt that the rite needed radical change and a general reappraisal. *The Times*, in a leader dated 5 May 1952, demanded revision of the whole coronation service in the light of developing needs and contemporary attitudes, not least social and political. It hoped that the ecclesiastical authorities would see that this was done.

A distinguished churchman, Dr Charles Raven, who became Vice-Chancellor of Cambridge University and was himself a scholar, naturalist and theologian, took this view, being reinforced in holding it by his conversations with many Canadians while in that country during the summer of 1952. He was convinced, he reported to the Archbishop, that something 'less archaic and domestic should now be designed'. 'I found out', he went on, 'the opinions strongly stated that on the last occasion the pageantry was wholly out of date and lacking in any sort of relevance to the world today.' The Archbishop's committee, however, was conservative – liturgical scholars usually are. However, the Duke of Edinburgh was firmly convinced that some such attempt should be made.

The participants in the rite were traditionally all Anglicans and the service, as we have seen, was framed within the Holy Communion. It was felt by many that to exclude the Moderator of the General Assembly of the Church of Scotland, the national church of that country, was wholly inexcusable, not least because the Sovereign herself became a Presbyterian north of the border. The Archbishop of Canterbury thought likewise and the Moderator, not inappropriately, was entrusted with the presentation of the Scriptures and saying the prescribed words. Thus a Scottish voice and accent was introduced into the Abbey.

As to the Commonwealth, some member states of which were monarchical, others republican, others only as yet in process of becoming independent, it seemed fitting, since the Queen was head of the Commonwealth, that they should have some part to play and that their inter-faith allegiance should be respected. One thing was quite clear, namely that the Archbishop of Canterbury in his capacity as titular head of the Anglican communion had no authority in a matter of this kind.

Sir Olaf Caroe, a distinguished civil servant with a long experience in India, made an eloquent plea to the Archbishop for a Commonwealth representation of some kind. As to the seven independent member states, it might be possible, he thought, for their governors-general to be given an active part when the Queen discarded St Edward's for the Imperial Crown, or failing this to revive the ancient ceremony in Westminster Hall which would give complete freedom of manoeuvre to do as one pleased.

Such participation, however, did not happen but it needs to be stressed that the failure to secure it was not due to any timid conservatism on the part of the Archbishop, though he was strongly opposed to reviving any ceremony in Westminster Hall on the grounds that it would devalue what was happening in the Abbey. Prompted by the Duke of Edinburgh, Geoffrey Fisher suggested the possibility that at the Recognition instead of asking the

'I'll put a girdle round about the earth in forty minutes,' so boasted Puck. But what is that to us. The BBC *engineers now do it in a seventh of a second.*

Unknown to fame, Mrs Jane Hill has a curious monument to her in the north aisle of the Nave. She kneels on a cushion unperturbed, with behind her a skeleton in a winding sheet.

same question four times the Archbishop might address different groups, for example, Sirs of the United Kingdom, Sirs of the Dominions, Sirs of the Colonial Empire. (Quite clearly women's 'lib' was not yet!)

The project in fact broke down because of what the Archbishop was told by Lord Swinton, Minister of State for the Commonwealth. It was 'hopeless', he said, to get Commonwealth countries to accept the changes proposed. They were already making difficulties about attendance. Pakistan was on the eve of declaring itself a republic. The view of the Dominions could be best expressed in these words: 'For heaven's sake don't go and create new problems when we have had such

difficulty in coming to agreement round the table about Style and Titles and other things.'

It was a matter of acute disappointment to Geoffrey Fisher that the Roman Catholic Archbishop of Westminster declined an invitation for his own or any Roman episcopal presence at the ceremony. In this he was following a precedent set at former coronations.

If the Roman Catholic hierarchy refused to attend there was one who, so far from being a suppliant for favours, might well in earlier years have been seated himself in the coronation chair. There were strong and responsible rumours that the Duke of Windsor was contemplating coming to England and that there would be a formal request for him to be allowed to attend. The Archbishop's reaction to this possibility was immediately that it would be 'wholly and entirely undesirable'. In this he was joined by the Queen's advisers. There followed 'off the record' consultations with the Duke's lawyers and the result was his being spared the experience which some have alleged, though almost certainly falsely, came the way of the Young Pretender at the coronation of George III.

There were many other matters demanding decision – for example, what part, if any, should be allocated to the Duke of Edinburgh, the more so as the Queen had specifically asked that he should be given one. The Archbishop felt strongly, whatever the difficulties, that some role should be found for him. Here precedents were few but it seemed worth while, if only some minor readjustments could be devised, to meet the Queen's request. Such, for example, were his walking behind the Sovereign at the processional entry; sitting on a fald-stool on her right; joining her as she received the Sacrament.

In addition, and here Geoffrey Fisher's own words may be quoted: 'I am entirely willing to forgo my claim that I have to do my Homage before anybody else. If Philip were merely a Royal Duke I should cling to my privileges, but [as] husband and next in precedence to the Queen, I think it is right to give way to him – although theoretically it means the Church consenting to act second to a layman.' In fact this was the solution agreed upon.

How extensive the use of television should be constituted a real problem and at the outset there were radical differences of opinion. The reasons for this were, firstly, the traditional one that certain aspects of the service were too sacred and personal to be exposed to general viewing – for example, the anointing and the reception of the Sacrament. 'Close-ups' here and the intense light needed could well prove an embarrassment to the Queen. Such scruples could be met only by a highly selective presentation such as by confining television to west of the choir screen. Those who took a contrary view stressed the enormous spiritual advantage of bringing the Coronation into the homes of ordinary citizens. This view prevailed for two reasons. The first was the steady persistence of the BBC and its Director General who, undaunted, built up a strong case for an extensive use of television which the Queen herself approved.

They were able to show that the lighting required was not excessive as used to be the case and that great restraint would be used throughout. This they demonstrated at rehearsals. The second reason was a forthright letter from the Prime Minister, Winston Churchill, to the Earl Marshal, urging that the BBC should be given full facilities.

So it was that the Coronation came to be televised more or less *in toto*. No one, in retrospect, could doubt that this decision was a right one and that it was not abused by the public. Some have called Elizabeth's crowning 'The Television Coronation' and the *New Statesman* made the same point with the caption to a cartoon: 'Richard Dimbleby ill: Coronation postponed.'

No coronation, it may be confidently claimed, was more thoroughly rehearsed than that of Queen Elizabeth in 1953. This was largely due to the happy cooperation of the Earl Marshal and the Archbishop, and of the Archbishop and the Director of Music, Dr William McKie. The latter had the full support of such men as Sir Arnold Bax and Sir Ralph Vaughan Williams. Doubtless it was this careful and dedicated preparation which made everything go so well on the day. There was a genuine atmosphere of reverence in the Abbey; and, as in the case of the youthful Victoria, Elizabeth, in and through her own oblation, associated with her a vast concourse both in the building and beyond. The Archbishop, if he lacked Cosmo Lang's capacity to lift the ceremony into a more transcendental dimension which left behind ordinary everyday experience, gave the Coronation a sense of purpose and efficiency which were near to godliness. There was no escape into another world but a commitment to fashion the here and now after the 'city that hath foundations'. Perhaps in this the Archbishop was helped by the very tensions and ambiguities built into nine hundred years of Abbey history.

One side-effect of the Coronation, and an important one, was that it brought the Archbishop more closely into touch with the Queen and other members of the Royal Family. He prepared for them a book of devotions relating to the basic meaning of the rite so that they could pray with the Queen till the great day came.

One memory of the Queen the Archbishop long treasured. It was at a rehearsal and the Queen was sitting in the coronation chair 'undisturbed'. He went up to her and they had a long conversation.

'She was quite on her own,' he wrote, 'with a look of real happiness on her face, and spoke enthusiastically of the Little Book saying that she was using it morning by morning in company with her family.' She welcomed the suggestion of a private rehearsal for the actual crowning. Of the final rehearsal he writes: 'She was at her absolute best – sincere, gay, happy, intensely interested, asking all the right questions about her movements and carrying them out very naturally and impressively.'

In the course of the preparations there were surprises. The Archbishop showed a great interest in the Royal Robes and supervised the unpacking of the chests containing those used at the Coronation of George VI. Alas! they would not do! Everyone had forgotten that the King was a man and the Queen was a woman!

It was impossible, of course, in so protracted and elaborate a ritual that some minor mistakes should not creep in. They did on this occasion, though the public must have been unaware of them. The Queen made her only blunder when she forgot the carefully rehearsed reverence as she entered the Choir at the beginning of the service. 'I was trying hard to will her to remember but failed. Neither supporting bishop liked to prompt her,' Dr Fisher wrote. The Archbishop also made a mistake in confusing the receiving of the armill with the reception of the sword, throwing his arms up in distress as he realized what he had done. Later the Queen told him that she was aware of his blunder and did her best to stop his moving at the wrong time. 'All square,' commented Dr Fisher.

The Chronicler of Westminster Abbey who was present in the Abbey confessed, to his own surprise, that the service, in spite of its archaic form, *did* communicate; and was, in its broad sweep, intelligible. Undoubtedly it all came alive in the pomp and circumstance, the glitter of the tiaras, the evocative beauty of the music, and the demeanour of the young Queen from beginning to end.

The Chronicler, however, observed that instead of those who swore their allegiance, most of whom once enjoyed but now had lost effective power, it would have been more realistic and in line with the intention of the rite if they had been replaced by others. Would it not be proper to ask where power *now* lies? And would not the answer be, for example, with such institutions as the Federation of British Industry, the Trades Union Congress and the media? Should we not now look here for those who are to swear their fealty? This does not mean that all tradition needs to be eliminated since the present is great with the past, only that it must not be so obtrusive as to create a sense of unreality.

In spite of earlier scepticism as to whether, after a period of great social change, the coronation would make any impact, the general verdict was that it had. Indeed it was followed by a mood of euphoria, so much so that suggestions were put forward as to there being an annual commemoration. However, Geoffrey Fisher shrewdly recognized that this, in practice, would lead to no end of difficulties. Who, for example, would decide when to stop it? Thus this proposal got no further, though the Archbishop spoke of its significance in an address at Westminster Abbey under the heading: 'Forward from the Coronation'.

The Abbey in its coronation setting looked fine and the Dean and Chapter of Westminster decided to commission Christopher Hassall to write a play or pageant to be performed there in the weeks following the ceremony. He responded with *Out of the Whirlwind*, a modern miracle play around a patriotic theme and using the history which this unique building provided. The cast, which included Fay Compton and Peter Coke, was excellent but the play did not, to use a modern vulgarism, 'gell'. To write against the background of the Abbey and in the national mood then obtaining would have set a problem for any contemporary playwright. Perhaps no other could have done better. I recall Christopher Hassall's distress when the *New Statesman* reviewed it under the caption: 'Mrs Dale sees it through'. There was more to the play than that!

Coronations are great national events and have contributed a unique feature to the Abbey. In life, however, benefits are often offset by corresponding disadvantages. This is certainly the case here. The elaborate preparations in the Abbey with the introduction of extra seating in tiers have led to more destruction than any other single cause. In this respect, coronations are wreckers, though fortunately more care is now taken. Would that it had been taken earlier!

NINE

Monuments and Memorials

IT IS an oft-repeated and standard complaint that Westminster Abbey is littered with monuments of various sorts, shapes, and sizes; that some of these are monstrosities; others outrageously large. Some are aesthetically pleasing, and others have great historical significance. At their worst they are at war with the building. Collectively they create an atmosphere unique to this Royal Peculiar. No one, perhaps, expresses this better than Francis Beaumont, friend of Ben Jonson who, with his brother, is buried at the entrance to St Benedict's Chapel:

> Mortality, behold and fear!
> What a change of flesh is here!
> Think how many royal bones
> Sleep within this heap of stones:
> Here they lie, had realms and lands,
> Who now want strength to stir their hands:
> Where from their pulpits seal'd with dust
> They preach, 'In greatness is no trust.'
> Here's an acre sown indeed
> With the richest royall'st seed
> That the earth did e'er suck in
> Since the first man died for sin:
> Here the bones of birth have cried –
> 'Though gods they were, as men they died.'
> Here are sands, ignoble things,
> Dropt from the ruin'd sides of kings;
> Here's a world of pomp and state,
> Buried in dust, once dead by fate.

Joseph Addison, who elected not to be buried in Poets' Corner but near his patron, confessed to the Earl of Halifax to walking, often in a serious mood, around the Abbey and reflecting:

When I see kings lying by those who deposed them, when I consider rival wits placed side by side, or the holy men that divided the world by their contests and disputes, I reflect with sorrow and astonishment on the little competitions, factions and debates of mankind. When I read the several dates of the tombs, of some that died yesterday, and some six hundred years ago, I consider that great day when we shall all of us be contemporaries, and make our appearance together.

There are many facets to this unique collection of statuary. People come to the Abbey who are engaged in specialized studies on English sculpture, its history and development; on heraldry, lettering, and English dress.

Like most things connected with the Abbey,

Edward III reigned fifty years, at first very successfully. He conquered both 'before his face and behind his back, whence he came and whither he went, north and south, one in his person, the other by his substitutes in his absence'. But his end was disastrous, and he was overwhelmed by the death of his son the Black Prince. He died deserted. Effigies of his fourteen children were on his tomb, but only six remain.

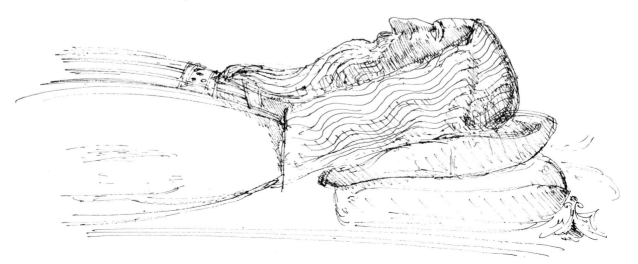

there has never been any consistent policy, implemented over the years, in respect of monuments and memorials. Maybe this is a good thing. The constitutional position now, though there have been disputes about this, the Dean and Chapter for a period being the authority, is that the Dean as Ordinary is empowered to decide whether permission be granted for a particular memorialization or burial. If he has any sense, and most Deans of Westminster have a modicum of it, he will not make a decision in response to what the philosopher Hare would call a 'blik'. Rather he will consult his colleagues on the Chapter who are properly described in the Statutes as 'senators'. He will also get into touch with many who are usually thought of as authorities in the specialized field in which the 'memorialee' is being considered. Always the desire is to seek something beyond even outstanding merit, rather excellence, high distinction to the point of genius. This is never

The fortunes of the Cecils were built up by the great Lord Burleigh, Queen Elizabeth's chief minister for many years. Of his eldest son, Thomas, appointed Earl of Exeter by James, was written: 'He was a person of very ordinary abilities, and if he had been born of other parentage we should have heard nothing of him'. Still, be this as it may, here he is with his first wife, pictured on a fine tomb. Thomas was not the first to suffer from a famous father!

easy to determine since judgements of this kind are often subjective as well as fallible and what is seen to qualify in one generation may appear polite, even commonplace in another. Still the hope and the expectation remain. One obvious way of avoiding mistakes is to eschew immediate memorialization and to allow time to pass its judgement. This sounds fine in theory but would hardly work in practice, for there is a certain historic value in recognizing contemporary distinction even if long years reverse it. There are, of course, fashions in literary taste. John Donne, the poet Dean of St Paul's memorialized in that Cathedral, has come into favour after many years of near total neglect. On the other hand who now reads Abraham Cowley, the child genius, whose 'Pyramus and Thisbe' was written at the age of ten and whose memorial in the South Transept is obtrusively gigantic? His great contemporary reputation has waned. Will it ever return?

One advantage of the Dean's prerogative in finally decreeing 'yea' or 'nay' in respect of memorialization is that it can lift decision-making out of politics and *force majeure*, that is if he is strong enough to resist pressure. No government can issue a diktat or require the Dean to act in a particular way. What is inevitably true is that this area of his duties can prove an embarrassing responsibility, as only those who have had to exercise it can know. Indeed it can impair friendships for this is a matter on which people feel deeply. Also decision-making in this area invades a territory where there are no absolutes.

What is important is that the whole process be kept confidential. It is never publicized that so and so is being considered for memorialization. Nor does rejection at one time mean rejection for all time. Shelley, Keats and Byron had to wait long years for recognition. Indeed, there was a society which existed for no other purpose than to secure Lord Byron's reception into the Abbey.

Here, however, I must add, and this is important, that once the Dean has made a decision to say 'yes', the character and location of the memorial are determined by the Dean and Chapter, quite apart from the fact that they hold the purse strings. Here they are advised by their own Surveyor of the Fabric, always a person of distinction and wide experience; also by an architectural advisory panel which contains a galaxy of talent in various relevant fields. This meets regularly and the Dean and

Benjamin Disraeli, who beside being a romantic, climbed 'the greasy pole' to become Prime Minister. His flattery of Queen Victoria, whom he made Empress of India, has gone down to history in his words: 'We authors, Ma'am,' referring to her Leaves from my Highland Diary.

Chapter take very serious account of what its members have to say though they are not bound by it. Often there are differences of view on the panel itself.

As with so much that characterizes the Abbey, neither the Benedictine monastery nor the Collegiate Church made a formal decision that this building should be a repository for memorials. It has become so across the centuries largely because of its national character and ongoing history. The number of memorials has in practice proved a problem, so much so as to provoke a public discussion (see p.103). Often to find room for a memorial there has been much wanton destruction inflicted upon the building, particularly on side chapels.

The first memorial in the Norman Abbey was Edward the Confessor's Shrine, made more glorious by Henry III in the new Gothic church which he built to his memory. It was natural that other

monarchs should wish their mortal remains to lie near to where Edward the Confessor was buried – and who more fitting than Henry III, second founder of the Abbey? Thus St Edward's Chapel began to be a place of royal burial for kings, queens and their children, though a bishop of Norwich, a friend of Henry V, was interred near the Shrine. And so the process went on, for ever enhancing the status of those either buried or memorialized within the church or in the Cloisters. In the course of time certain areas in the Abbey developed particular associations – for example, Poets' Corner, the Statesmen's and Musicians' Aisles – but in many cases memorializations were *ad hoc* and undifferentiated. An attempt was made some years ago to introduce a little systematization in the Nave. The stone floor there is now falling victim to the relentless tread of millions of feet. It will at some point have to be replaced. In the sixties it was determined to grasp this nettle and the Surveyor of the Fabric was asked to take this matter in hand. He accordingly drew up a remarkably fine design for a Cosmati marble floor in coloured stone which in its intricate weaving of individual patterns was an aesthetic delight. One of the snags, unfortunately, was that it demanded, if the overall pattern were to be consistently respected, the removal and resiting of many memorials. Plans were therefore drawn up to do this by bringing together memorials of deans, of prime ministers and statesmen, to mention but a few categories.

This scheme, however, for a number of reasons, one being a change in the Minister for the Arts, was never implemented. The Dean of Westminster, Dr Eric Abbott, took it to the Palace where, we are told, it received the comment that its uniformity suggested 'symmetry in a cemetery'. Thus the design, looking, in my judgement, as attractive and satisfying as ever, remains as a muniment in the Library.

Poets' Corner, which is known the world over – another has recently been installed in St John's Cathedral, New York – only gradually established itself, largely under the impetus of that amazing outburst of literary and more than literary genius during the first Elizabethan age. England and the English language, through the cross-fertilization of the Teutonic and the Romance, had at last come of age and found themselves. Geoffrey Chaucer, buried in the South Transcept was now given a more worthy tomb and Edmund Spenser was laid to rest near him. 'Rare' Ben Jonson's body was interred four days after his death on the north side of the Nave of the Abbey. An elaborate tomb was contemplated for him in 1638 when thirty eulogies by leading poets were published under the title *Jonsonus Virbius*. But this scheme petered out and it was left to a casual visitor, Sir John Young, to cause the words 'O Rare Ben Jonson' to be cut in the stone, and for the Earl of Oxford to put a monument with a portrait bust on the south wall of Poets' Corner. But still those who could afford it, though lacking any literary pretensions, crept into Poets' Corner. Fines for such memorials went into the pockets of members of the Dean and Chapter!

The Statesmen's Aisle in the North Transept is mostly confined to outstanding nineteenth-century politicians, who discharged their offices during the full flood of Empire. There stands Stratford Canning and near him those great rivals Gladstone and Disraeli, the former evoking from Queen Victoria the criticism that he treated her like a public meeting, the latter more subtly wooing her with his 'We authors, ma'am'. (She

The Statesmen's Aisle, now that the shooting and the tumult has died and the captains and the kings have departed, perpetrates the golden age of empire and the self-confidence of the Victorians.

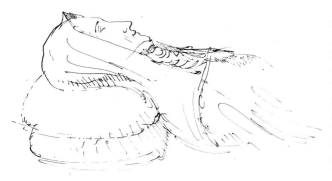

Lady Margaret Beaufort, mother of King Henry VII, is incapsulated in this most beautiful bronze effigy, full of repose and quiet serenity, executed by the Italian craftsmen, Torrigiani. The pose and poise, so well portrayed, subdue and quieten the external noise of many visitor's feet. Her hands have been described as 'the most perfect in Christendom'.

had in fact written one book in two volumes, *Leaves from my Highland Diary* and *More Leaves from my Highland Diary*.)

It is curious how unpleasing, as in the Statesmen's Aisle, it seems when in a church the 'memorialee' stands upright on a pedestal. It suggests arrogance, and the deification of man. How different it is with Margaret Beaufort, mother of Henry VII, who died in the Abbot's House on 29 June 1509, St Peter's Day, and of whom Erasmus said, so beautifully: 'Everyone that knew her loved her and everything that she said or did became her.' Her bronze recumbent effigy by Torrigiani at the east end of the south aisle of Henry VII's Chapel is a masterpiece. Everything is right and in character – her widow's dress with a hood and long mantle, her feet on a hind couchant, and her delicate, wrinkled hands raised in prayer. How many must have contemplated her effigy across the centuries and drawn from it spiritual comfort. 'She being dead yet speaketh.'

In the same way, though the genre, of course, is entirely different, the bust by Epstein of William Blake in Poets' Corner is so alive as to make a great deal of the statuary surrounding it seem polite and pedestrian. Epstein has managed to give expression to the fire of Blake's consuming vision. (How much more romantic, by the way, Tennyson looks without his beard!)

Again, what a remarkable contrast between Lady Margaret's restrained piety and the flamboyant 'folly', a technical masterpiece, erected to the

memory of Baron Hunsdon at the east end of St John the Baptist's Chapel. It is some thirty-six feet in height, with Corinthian columns, a glitter of colour and patterned stone, a very riot of inventiveness and Renaissance extravagance. The cost must have been astronomical even for those days and perhaps that is why Hunsdon was buried in Westminster Abbey at the Queen's expense, but it was his widow who erected the monument over his tomb. No one could accuse the Virgin Queen – Hunsdon was her cousin – of extravagance. Indeed he thought he had a very raw deal from his relative, for when at the end of his life she sought to make him an earl he declined the honour on the grounds that if she had deemed him unworthy of it in his lifetime it ill became him to accept it on his deathbed.

Scientists are now increasingly being memorialized, beginning with the quite remarkable monument to Sir Isaac Newton – testimony to the high regard in which he was universally held at his death, which Alexander Pope encapsulated in his famous couplet:

> Nature and nature's laws lay hid in night;
> God said, *Let Newton be!* and all was light.

Newton's prominent memorial, executed by Rysbrack, led to the entry of the astronomers, the Herschels, father and son, who have been joined in the Cloisters by Edmond Halley who collaborated with Sir Isaac Newton.

Visitors may well be surprised to discover how many singers, actors, actresses and dramatists, in the main from the seventeenth and eighteenth centuries, have been memorialized and buried in the Abbey. Amongst these are Anne Oldfield (whose body lay in state in Jerusalem Chamber), Bess Saunderson, Thomas Betterton, David Garrick, Richard Sheridan, Sir Henry Irving, Jenny Lind and a host of others.

Recently there have been two memorializations in the south choir aisle: Sybil Thorndike and Noel Coward. In respect of the former it was decided to introduce some doggerel verse on to the memorial such as adorned many memorials in years gone by. This was secured, with his very kind permission, by shortening a verse tribute which appeared in *Punch* and was written by J. B. Priestley for Dame Sybil's eightieth birthday. The changes made were radical, but basically the verse is his. The first lines run:

> St Joan or Hecuba,
> Great Actress of your age,
> All woman-hood your part,
> The World your stage.

The tribute to Noel Coward will long be remembered by those present in the Abbey at his memorial service. It was an occasion of vivid contrasts – traditional to begin with and then suddenly there burst forth his music full of haunting melodies and nostalgia. The stone bears a brief inscription: 'A talent to amuse'.

My hope is that the south Choir Aisle will be set apart for actors and the theatre generally. Certainly the stage is a great art form and is one in which Britain has excelled.

Efforts have been made over the years to engage in a little pruning of the memorials, usually those of excessive awkwardness and size. The gigantic statue of James Watt in marble, executed by Chantrey, was removed from St Paul's Chapel in December 1960 to the Transport Commission's Museum then at Clapham. So massive was it that even to get the pedestal into the Chapel originally meant dividing it into three pieces, dragging it over Lewis Robessart's (Lord Bourgchier's) tomb, and in the process destroying the ancient coffin lid. The statue itself had to be forced through the door, but the vaulting gave way, revealing row upon row of gilded coffins. If to get the monument into the Chapel was difficult it was no more easy to get it out. Fortunately its replacement was a more simple plaster bust presented by the Institute of Mechanical Engineers.

The monuments to Nicholas Rowe, poet laureate and Shakespearean scholar, and John Gay of *The Beggar's Opera* fame who coined the phrase 'Where there is life there's hope', have been removed to the triforium which means that Rysbrack's representations of Rowe and Gay are no longer visible to the public. The reason for this removal was to reveal permanently two thirteenth-century wall paintings, representing St Christopher and St Thomas, which the two monuments concealed. The obscurity given to these paintings is a typical example of the insensitivity of the eighteenth century to anything that smacked of the medieval period. Alexander Pope described Gay as 'In wit a man; simplicity a child'. On his monu-

Baron Hunsdon, cousin of Queen Elizabeth, a spendiferous, gigantic, extravagant, Renaissance 'folly'.

The Duke of Buckingham, George Villiers, a favourite of Prince Charles whom he accompanied to Spain in a fruitless effort to promote a royal marriage by wooing the Infanta. It will be seen that terrible destruction resulted from the difficult task of placing the memorial in situ. 'His (George Villier's) ascent was so quick that it seemed rather a flight than a growth.'

ment, at his own request, is a flippant quotation from a letter he wrote to Pope, because it signified 'his present sentiment'.

> Life is a jest; and all things show it.
> I thought so once; but now I know it.

However, removing a monument from display in the Abbey is no simple matter. Before this is done it is usual to seek the permission of the head of the family if such can be found. It proved impossible to move the immense memorial to Lord Mansfield, the famous judge, from the North Transept, in spite of the fact that he left a clause in his will that on no account should there be any public memorial erected in his memory. It was Lord Mansfield who made the famous declaration that once a slave reached these shores he became free.

Fashions and forms of memorialization change in response to contemporary manners and *mores*. The Abbey demonstrates this fact. Medieval memorials often depict the departed in a recumbent position and the inscription is in Latin. Elizabethans often preferred a higher personal identity with the 'memorialee' on his knees. Inhibitions, doubtless begotten from some vestigial but built-in religious approach, ceased to restrain in the late seventeenth and eighteenth centuries. Busts were common; the person memorialized could be shown in a variety of poses; inscriptions were often long, eulogistic and tedious as for Charles Godolphin and his wife in the West Cloister, the latter being the foundress of the Godolphin School in Salisbury whose pupils visit the Abbey on their anniversary day. An admiral could be depicted with his ship even though he was responsible for plunging it to the bottom of the ocean.

The twentieth century has introduced much more restraint in response to an increasing demand: 'No more statues or busts *please*.' Yet in acceding to this request the Abbey has run into difficulty. The tendency has been to memorialize almost exclusively on the floor or to place a small tablet on the wall, though there are exceptions – General Booth, for example, has a bust in St George's, the Warrior's Chapel, near the West Door. In Poets' Corner most of the more recent memorials have a sameness about them – white lettering on black stone with a short, but, it is hoped, telling quotation, typifying the person thus honoured. One advantage of this particular style is easy legibility, but many now feel that this has been grossly overdone, that the prospect of an increasingly black floor is depressing, lacking in variety and imagination. It might be argued that the highest compliment is simply to record the name of the person memorialized, as in the case of Shelley and Keats, but this does little to interest the vast majority of visitors whose literary background is meagre to say the least and many of whom are not English. The short but pregnant quotation may well linger in the memory.

There is a great deal in Westminster Abbey which calls powerful attention to the grim fact of war. The visitor on entry at the West Door if he glances backwards and then upwards will see a statue of the great William Pitt, Prime Minister during the Napoleonic wars, whose last words wrung from him on hearing the news of the Battle of Austerlitz were: 'Oh, my country, how I leave my country!' Ahead on the floor the sightseer is confronted by a large memorial to Winston Churchill who led Britain during the Second World War; and separated by a mere matter of a few feet is the Grave of the Unknown Warrior which still evokes in many of the millions who see it thoughts 'too deep for tears'. At the east end of the Abbey in the Royal Air Force Chapel is the Battle of Britain window designed by Hugh Easton, a skilful blend of patterns in colour which include RAF badges commemorating 'the few'. In the centre of the Nave is a memorial to the most daring of admirals, Lord Cochrane, who played a prominent part in helping to secure the independence of Greece, Chile, Brazil and Peru. Once a year the HMS Barham Survivors Association come to the Abbey to remember their comrades drowned when their ship was torpedoed in the Mediterranean in 1941. Also in the Nave is a memorial recording the names of the fallen who belonged to the Queen's Westminsters. Once a year wreaths are laid in the Royal Air Force Chapel on the graves of Air Chief Marshal Lord Dowding and Marshal of the RAF Viscount Trenchard.

The Earl of Mansfield, lord chief justice of England –
'The oracle of the law, the standard of eloquence and the pattern of virtue'.

This is the tomb of Richard II and Anne of Bohemia seen from the South Ambulatory. Richard was devoted to the Abbey where his coronation was more magnificent than any of his predecessors'. He bravely quelled Watt Tyler's rebellion; but in 1399 he was deposed by his cousin, Henry of Lancaster, and was subsequently either murdered or died because he starved himself. His portrait hangs in the Nave.

It may well be that the reaction of some people is to question whether such memorializations should be so prominent in a church whose prime responsibility is to mediate the Christian Gospel. One can understand this caveat since the violence of war is at odds with God's perfect kingdom no matter how praiseworthy are the courage and gallantry of those who take part in it. But my theme throughout these somewhat scattered reflections is that the Abbey bears witness to the built-in tension between the two kingdoms, between the city that hath the foundations and the cities that we fitfully build. Are not these symbolically represented in the contrast between St Edward the Confessor and William the Conqueror? I personally am always conscious of this dilemma when I see the cannons on a memorial at the west end of the Nave. I am, I confess, ill at ease. (I have been requested more than once to secure their removal!) Yet I should not react this way if I saw such weaponry in the Imperial War Museum; and I would not do so because the Abbey is a church and as such must always see itself as under the judgement of God, that is under the constraint of those 'impossible possibilities' of the Sermon on the Mount to which Reinhold Niebuhr, the theologian, calls attention. It would be more comfortable to withdraw from this embarrassing and agonizing tension and to consecrate all that the state does: or to retreat into an ivory tower of self-righteous superiority unheeding of the world. Neither is right and neither has commended itself to the Abbey, though it is

increasingly being accepted that absolute war is absolutely out, and that our thinking in these areas in the light of an entirely new situation demands a radical reappraisal of the ethics of war.

A service was held here to mark the thirtieth anniversary of the North Atlantic Treaty Organization when the Bishop of Durham, now the Archbishop of York, gave a closely reasoned address which endeavoured to face up to the complexities of today. Also the Abbey held a service to mark the fortieth anniversary of the end of the war in Europe at which the Archbishop of Canterbury, Dr Runcie, preached with equal openness and deep conviction. It was a memorable occasion. Present were representatives of Churches east and west of the Iron Curtain; from Russia, America, East and West Germany and Japan. The service began with a moving tribute to the fallen and a remembrance of those who still bear the scars of war together with those who mourn. It moved on to the theme of reconciliation; and then to the rekindling of the undying, visionary hope that God's kingdom will come and the human family enter into its destined inheritance. This was movingly depicted by some forty-odd young boys and

Three sea captains killed in a naval battle off the coast of the West Indies. Britannia surveys them approvingly.

girls from the Royal Ballet School who processed up the central aisle laying flowers in the form of a cross before the High Altar. While this was being done a schoolgirl read the ancient prophecy:

> They shall beat their swords into plough shares
> And their spears into pruning hooks
> Nation shall not lift up sword against nation
> Neither shall they learn war any more.

After the service all the participants adjourned to the Deanery for lunch. As the children walked along the gallery they were given a rousing and vociferous reception. The Archbishop of Canterbury, the Cardinal Archbishop of Westminster and the Metropolitan of Leningrad spoke to us. May this service prove a happy augury of the shape of things to come.

I now turn to an event on the eve of my departure from the Abbey. I often used to encourage my colleagues with the words: 'Look up for your redemption draweth nigh', which gave me personally unique pleasure and satisfaction. For some considerable time I made myself a bore at dinner parties by asking a fellow guest, if he seemed promising in this context, 'If you were to memorialize in Westminster Abbey a group of First World War poets – that is poets who at the time wrote about war – who would they be?' It was amazing how in the end the choice crystallized around some sixteen. (I consulted others, of course, besides fellow guests at dinners!) So this memorialization eventually took place. The sixteen names were incised on a stone placed in Poets' Corner and bearing words by Wilfred Owen: 'My subject is War, and the pity of War. The poetry is in the pity.' Extracts were read from the sixteen, and it was significant to notice the change of mood from the romantic to the patriotic and finally to cynicism and near-despair. Michael Howard, Regius Professor of Modern History at Oxford, gave the address, one of the finest I have heard at the Abbey, which concluded with these solemn words:

So the Great War poets remain unique; unique in the quality of their diction; unique in the tragic intensity of their message. Their suffering has passed into our common experience, and has enlarged our common understanding. After they wrote, no one could ever think of war in the same way again; and they thus made it

The Crossing from the Muniment Room.

Rear Admiral Charles Holmes served in Jamaica. Here he is depicted as a Roman soldier.

less likely that there ever *would* be war again. Out of the furnace of battle they told us what war is like. They achieved the object of all great art. They told us the truth. That is why we honour them today.

Few deny that many monuments and plaques have been 'inserted with a ruthless disregard for the architectural design'; some ought never to have gained entry at all. Public interest became such in the late nineteenth century that two royal commissions met to deal with this problem, and proposals were put forward for monuments to be housed in a hall or cloisters linked closely to the Abbey itself. The plans for doing this, including drawings by Sir Gilbert Scott and John Pearson, are still in existence but were never carried out.

Each of the monuments in the Abbey has its own story to tell. Perhaps I may be allowed to comment on two which interest me in particular. These are the memorials to Elizabeth, wife of John Warren, Bishop of Bangor and to Dorothy Osborne in the Nave.

It is always good to read of an eighteenth-century bishop who used his talents with pastoral insight and integrity and it was from a deep

Good, loveable and kindly Mrs Warren: 'The quality of mercy is not strain'd. It droppeth as the gentle rain from Heaven upon the place beneath'.

concern that John Warren wrote in 1785, *The Duties of the Parochial Clergy*. His wife was equally exemplary and, making allowance for excessive adulation to which memorial inscriptions are too often prone, it is clear that the high reputation she enjoyed was deserved. 'She was', it records, 'distinguished for the purity of her taste, and the soundness of her judgement. Her prudence and discrimination were in no instances more conspicuous than in selecting the objectives of her extensive charity. The widow and the fatherless were protected and relieved and the virtuous who had fallen from prosperity had peculiar claims to her benevolence.' There is a great deal of polite statuary in the Abbey which, technically flawless, means little: but this monument to good Mrs Warren, erected by her sister, is different. With great sensitivity and delicacy of feeling there is depicted a young girl with her baby, complete with her begging bowl. Many who view it may think of the Madonna for whom there was no room at the inn.

Many years ago I was given for a Christmas present an Everyman edition of *Dorothy Osborne's Letters*. I took it with me on a journey up to London. It fascinated me to such an extent that when I got to Waterloo Station I spent the rest of the day reading it in a waiting room. Her letters, written during the period of the Civil War to her fiancé, William Temple, have a restraint and sensitivity truly delightful. When I discovered that Dorothy was memorialized in the Abbey, I was thrilled. It was like meeting up again with an old and dear friend.

I am inclined to end this chapter with a challenge to the reader. Some of you must know Walter Savage Landor's *Imaginary Conversations of Literary Men and Statesmen*. Would it not be an attractive exercise for someone to set the occupants of Poets' Corner talking to one another, say, during the night hours when they take over the Abbey?

The mere existence of Poets' Corner in the Abbey calls powerful attention to the significance of this great art form and the richness of the English language. 'Poets are the trumpets which sing to battle . . . the unacknowledged legislators of the world.'

KEATS   SHELLEY

ROBERT SOUTHEY

GULIELMO SHAKESPEARE
ANNO...

JOHNSON

JANE
AUSTEN

WILLIAM SHAKESPEARE 1564-1616

TEN

Two Nineteenth-Century Deans

THERE WERE many conscientious and good Deans of Westminster during the nineteenth century. Two of them were outstanding and we turn to them – Deans Buckland and Stanley.

There can be no doubt that William Buckland, Dean of Westminster from 1845 to 1856, became increasingly eccentric in his latter years, which led to many stories being told about him, some doubtless apocryphal but in character. This is unfortunate since it has tended to draw attention away from his considerable achievements as a scientist and equally as Dean of Westminster. I will begin with two anecdotes about him, probably not apocryphal, before turning to his solid work and worth.

Buckland early developed the habit, in his researches, of submitting himself to eating a variety of foods not contained in a normal diet. In early days this was doubtless kept under control, but one instance, late in life, has become legendary. Buckland was in Islip, the birthplace of Edward the Confessor, being entertained in the manor house. The host was a descendant of the British Ambassador in Paris when the royal tombs were despoiled. Somehow, as a consequence, there came into his possession the heart of Louis XIV. This curious relic was kept in a silken handkerchief and, as happened with the poet Shelley's heart, it powdered. At dinner this unique exhibit was passed round the table. When it came to Buckland he held the handkerchief to his lips, put the contents into his mouth, and said solemnly: 'See, I am eating the heart of *le roi soleil* before whom all Europe trembled.'

The other story relates to a journey which Buckland undertook with a friend, both on horseback, from Islip to London. Before they arrived at journey's end darkness descended and the Dean's somewhat worried companion protested that they were lost. 'Wait a moment,' said Buckland, jumping down from his horse. Then he knelt down, smelt the ground and replied reassuringly, 'Uxbridge'.

Having got this aspect of his character out of the way, let us consider Buckland in a more serious context.

Buckland was the son of a country parson in Devonshire and in his earliest days he explored his native heath researching into its natural phenomena. From Blundell's School in Tiverton and Winchester College he went up to Corpus Christi College at Oxford, where after taking his degree he became a fellow of his College and was ordained.

Throughout life Buckland believed that it was possible, arguing from the universe and its order, to infer the existence of God. However, at this stage in his life, mineralogy became his chief interest, indeed passion, and he travelled extensively on horseback over south-west England, collecting geological material and organic remains. In 1813 he followed Dr Kidd, the first physician in Oxford to lay aside the traditional wig and hat, in the chair of mineralogy. He later moved to a chair in geology. For the next thirty years he worked unceasingly in this field, producing innumerable papers, all of them illuminated by his first-hand investigations shot through with a scientific yet imaginative approach. He was undoubtedly, for a period of years, the leading geologist in the country and this was recognized by his being made a Fellow of the Royal Society and a President of the Royal Geological Society. Perhaps his greatest single work was his contributing a Bridgwater Treatise in 1836 in which he endeavoured to prove by the aid of science how extensively the 'Power, Wisdom and the Goodness of God are manifested in the Creation' – certainly an ambitious task. 'The whole course of the inquiry,' he wrote, 'which we have now conducted to its close, has shown that the physical history of our globe, in which some have seen only waste, disorder, and confusion teems

The Deanery, formerly the Abbot's lodgings and one of the oldest private houses still lived in. It has a long gallery, about the length of a cricket pitch. In this house Bishop Atterbury plotted treason.

ROBERT PEEL

with endless examples of economy and order, and design.' He does not seem to have worried overmuch at the predatory habits of animals as a condition of the species' survival! Perhaps it was a pity, in many respects, that Buckland was writing before a critical approach to the Bible had really got off the ground or Charles Darwin's researches had become current.

A dramatic change was brought about in the pattern of Buckland's life when Sir Robert Peel appointed him to the Deanery of Westminster in 1845, following Samuel Wilberforce who went off as Bishop of Oxford within a year of his holding this office. Buckland was delighted at the move, and with his wife kept open house at the Deanery. Distinguished scientists came there for serious conversation, and a constant stream of visitors also enjoyed the Bucklands' hospitality over breakfast or lunch. He threw himself into all that he did with real enthusiasm, even to investigating the foundations of the Abbey, thus reassuringly convincing himself that it was built on 'a peninsula of the purest sand and gravel'.

In May 1848 Buckland and two of his daughters were attacked with typhoid, or Westminster fever as it was known, since it seldom went beyond the Precincts. Several deaths occurred and the tolling of the Abbey bell was constant. He himself now took the initiative in applying his scientific knowledge to effect a thorough cleansing of the site. Some 400 cubic yards of foul matter was removed from the various branches of the ancient sewers which had silted up. The system of pipe drainage, which he introduced, was the first of its kind ever provided in London. Nor did he confine his interest to Westminster. As an active member of the Institution of Civil Engineers he concerned himself with the supply of pure water for the Metropolis and examined carefully the possible sources of supply for this.

On 15 November 1849 he preached in the Abbey at a service of thanksgiving for the removal of the cholera, taking as his text the prophet's words to Naaman, 'Wash and be clean'. No one could have been more forthright than Buckland in condemning the irresponsibility of many a local landlord. 'The greater number of the poor who perish are

Sir Robert Peel, Prime Minister, founder of the modern police force (hence bobby); promoter of Catholic emancipation; repealer of the Corn Laws.

the victims of the avarice and neglect of small landlords and owners of the filthy, ill-ventilated habitations in which the poorest and most ill-fed and helpless are compelled to dwell. Fatal diseases are continually engendered from lack of adequate supplies of water, withholden from the dwellings of the poor by the negligence of the owners.' It would be the fault of Parliament 'if we do not instantly begin to remedy these crying evils, if in two or three years our city is not duly supplied with water. Above all things, cleanse your hearts and not your garments only, and turn unto the Lord your God.'

Not every Dean of Westminster, one suspects, would be so forthright and outspoken on a matter of this kind in the pulpit of the Abbey. Buckland's interests were exceptionally wide, and the energy with which he pursued them constant. Thus he was present at the opening of some Anglo-Saxon barrows at Breachdown near Canterbury, examining in particular the flattened and polished surfaces of the warriors' molar teeth. On another occasion he made an intense examination of the claw of an eagle and the bones of other birds which he himself unearthed on the site of a Roman villa near Weymouth.

Along with his technical, scientific concerns he threw himself into ministering to the spiritual needs of the poor in Westminster until illness overtook him; then Mrs Buckland took over. The parish of St Matthew was inaugurated at this time and Mrs Buckland set up a coffee house in Pye Street which was combined with an industrial school where boys were taught to make paper bags and to print. This complex was the first of its kind in London and was modelled on a previous one in Edinburgh.

Dean Buckland usually spent the autumn at Islip where he was Rector. He provided allotments for the labourers and directed how they should be laid out. In 1846 famine crept over England and Buckland was active in persuading the villagers to make loaves of barley, grown on their own allotments. He supplied the village shops with sacks of hominy and Indian meal. He also built a cottage at the end of the old tithe barn where he fitted out one room for the recreation of village boys.

Buckland was lively, even at breakfast time, and the life and soul of many a party, doing things his own way, very different from the academic image which he might have been expected to project. Sir

A weeper on the tomb of Aymer de Valence, Earl of Pembroke. His second wife, Mary, founded Pembroke College, Oxford.

Roderick Murchison, referring to a meeting of the British Association at Bristol, writes to a friend: 'At that meeting the fun of the evening was a lecture of Buckland's. In that part of his discourse which treated of ichnolites or fossil footprints, the Doctor exhibited himself as a cock or a hen on the edge of a muddy pond, making impressions by lifting one leg after another. Many of the grave people thought our science was altered to buffoonery by an Oxford Don.'

Dean Buckland came to the Abbey when Edward Blore, the Surveyor of the Fabric, had completely redesigned the Choir and Transepts so that they were able to seat six hundred, all of whom could see and hear the officiating ministers, which certainly was not the case in the Nave. He preached a sermon 'On the occasion of the re-opening of the Choir and the Application of the Transepts to the Reception of the Congregation'. The background of this discourse was the Chartist agitation at home and revolutions abroad which prompted him to consider a wider national and international scene, using his scientific researches to point a moral. What he said could not have given pleasure or satisfaction to any Chartists had they been present – which they almost certainly were not! To many of them, in spite of the witness of such as F.D.Maurice with his Christian socialism, the Church was the enemy. 'There never was and, while human nature remains the same, there never can be a period in the history of human society when inequalities of worldly conditions will not follow the unequal use of talents and opportunities originally the same. . . . Equality of mind or body, or of worldly condition is as inconsistent with the order of nature as with the moral laws of God.' So says Buckland.

One can almost hear Mrs Thatcher saying a devout *Amen*.

Such a thesis – it falls short of Adam Smith's near economic determinism – does not gainsay the fact that Buckland possessed a very compassionate heart: what it does show is how profound was the effect upon him of his researches into a nature 'red in tooth and claw'. It says much for Buckland that he worked consistently to remove such inequalities as led to rank injustice, poverty and frustration. At the end of the day he was on the side of the angels and a very practical man to boot.

When Buckland reached his seventies, his health dramatically declined, leaving him unable to work effectively and subject to great fits of depression. The doctors were mystified and could not help him, though hoping that as the cause was unknown so he might, equally mysteriously, recover. It was only after his death – he died on 14 August 1856 – that an autopsy showed that the portion of the base of the skull on which the brain rested, together with the two upper vertebrae of the neck, were in an advanced state of decay. Apparently this was the result of an accident many years earlier on the Continent when a diligence overturned.

Buckland was buried at the west end of the churchyard in Islip, the Sub-Dean of Westminster, Lord John Thynne, inscribing on his memorial stone:

> Endued with superior Intellect,
> He applied the Powers of his Mind
> To the Honour and Glory of God,
> The advancement of Science
> And the welfare of Mankind.

Mrs Buckland was later interred in the same grave. Their son wrote: 'A simple but lasting monument of polished Aberdeen granite records the last resting place of as good a man and wife as ever did their duty towards God and towards their fellow creatures.' One cannot say more!

Of all the nineteenth-century deans, Arthur Penrhyn Stanley was the most sensitive to the historical ethos of the Abbey and the opportunities which it gave him, as Dean, to advance the kingdom of God in various areas of the national life. His father, who became Bishop of Norwich, sent him to Rugby School where he fell under the spell of the great Arnold who remained the single most formative influence, the 'lodestar', of his life. He both loved and venerated him to the point where it became almost a cause for anxiety. 'I always felt that this happiness is a dangerous one,' he wrote, 'and that loving and admiring him as I do to the very verge of all love and admiration that can be paid to man, I fear I have passed the limit and made him my idol, and that in all I may be but serving God for man's sake.' Not surprisingly, his biography of Arnold, which he undertook in his twenties, is probably the best book that he ever wrote. From Rugby he went up to Balliol College, Oxford, where he became Ireland scholar and a Newdigate prize winner; also a Fellow of University College where he gained further awards. He became ordained but, significantly, only after prolonged hesitation because of the condemnatory clauses in the Athansian Creed to which a clergyman was then required to give assent. He kept up a life-long struggle, and in 1865 was successful, to secure relief for the clergy from the stringent terms of the articles of subscription to which they must pledge themselves. In 1856 he was appointed Professor of Ecclesiastical History and a Canon of Christ Church. For a brief time he felt the 'strong influence of Newmanism' but this phase soon passed.

Travel, which he began in his schooldays, grew to become a major interest, which ministered to something deep-seated in his make-up. Almost every year he set out on his voyages of discovery, which across the years included the Holy Land, Europe, Asia, Africa, and America. From these there resulted a series of books of which *Sinai and Palestine* (1856) was almost certainly the best. It was historical places and people which moved him more than beauties of landscape and the majesty of mountains.

Stanley was unhappy at the divisive religious debates going on at Oxford during the 1830s and 40s, and when Arnold's return to Oxford in 1841 as Professor of Modern History was followed soon afterwards by his death, Stanley was shattered. It was for him an unrelieved tragedy, serving to confirm in him the general religious approach which he learnt from Arnold and which he was to hold with deep conviction across the years. To be tolerant of divergent views was almost part of his gospel. Hence he opposed alike the degradation of W. G. Ward for his pro-Roman sympathies and the agitation against the latitudinarian Dr Hampden before his appointment in 1848 to the bishopric of Hereford. (The Dean of Hereford in dismay wrote to Lord John Russell protesting that he would, on the Chapter, vote against Dr Hampden's election. The noble lord replied: 'Sir, I have had the honour to receive your letter of the 25th instant in which you intimate to me your intention of violating the law.') Without sympathizing with the views of either, Stanley condemned the indiscriminate clamour with which Evangelicals and High Churchmen assailed each other. Thus while acknowledging the debt he owed to Arnold, Stanley came to recognize what he himself owed to German theologians.

Arthur Penrhyn Stanley, most distinguished and effective of the nineteenth-century deans, has a recumbent effigy in Henry VII Chapel. No memorialization of this kind has taken place since – nor is it likely to.

Stanley's interests were not confined to ecclesiastical affairs. To his critics in England he was identified with political and university reform. Also he wrote extensively on biblical subjects including a history of the Jewish Church.

Informing all his works there was an emphasis on the practical side of life rather than on the formal statements of creeds; and this applied to his assessment of such controversial works as *Essays and Reviews*. He was no academic recluse nor did his instincts lead him that way. In 1862 he accompanied the Prince of Wales on a tour in the East. This introduced him intimately into the circles of the Royal Family, in particular to Queen Victoria, and to Lady Augusta Bruce whose brother died while accompanying them on the tour and whom Stanley married in the Abbey three days before Christmas in 1863. Stanley's connection with Queen Victoria meant that as she increasingly got to know him so she frequently consulted him on matters connected with the Church. He was always at hand and it is not hard to guess what kind of advice he gave her.

On 9 January 1864, through the instrumentality of Lord Palmerston, Stanley was installed as Dean of Westminster. In nearly all respects the Abbey was to give him everything that he could have wished for, though his first introduction and welcome left much to be desired. His reputation had gone before him and did not commend him universally to those he was to work with.

Canon Christopher Wordsworth, a High Churchman, conspicuously if conscientiously absented himself from the new Dean's installation. Not content with this absenteeism he also preached against him from the Abbey pulpit and published a pamphlet condemning his views. To his wife, Stanley characteristically confided: 'Perhaps it [Wordsworth's sermon] is to be answered by a calm reply, certainly by an invitation to dinner.' His first impression of meeting his new colleagues on the Chapter was disappointing, as a further letter to Augusta makes only too evident:

I confess that I felt no elation, nothing but depression, at the prospect before me. It seemed to me as if I were going down alive into the sepulchre. I had a long conversation with Lord J. Thynne, very courteous and sensible, but opening a vista of interminable questions of the most uninteresting kind ... as far as the actual work of the Dean is concerned, it is far more unsuited to me than that of a bishop. To lose one's time in conversations is bad, but to lose it in leases and warming [i.e. heating] plans is worse. However, the deed is done, and my useful life I consider to be closed, except so far as I can snatch portions from the troubles of the office.

Never was a man more mistaken! These gloomy forebodings proved to have no foundation. It is true that Stanley was neither a financier nor an administrator, nor was he expected to be at any level of high expertise. Indeed the Abbey inherited from its medieval past specific officers to undertake particular responsibilities under the Dean and Chapter. True, if these were to prove inadequate the Dean would need to do something about it as did Abbot Islip centuries earlier. It was perhaps unfortunate that Stanley should have come to the Abbey when two very pressing and supremely important matters were under discussion and waiting for a decision. One related to Abbey finances, the other to the status of Westminster School.

The Abbey was on the verge of bankruptcy and unable to meet its commitments. Doubtless it was this situation which caused the Sub-Dean great anxiety and which he felt he ought immediately to share with the new Dean. At about the same time, Dean Stanley came in for another and equally difficult problem. This arose out of the Dean and Chapter surrendering their extensive estates to the Church Commissioners in 1868 in return for an annual income of £20,000. It is usually agreed, with hindsight, that this sum was ludicrously small, and even in pre-inflationary days inadequate. Lord John Thynne, a former Treasurer, was opposed to the deal but Chapter authorized it, a decision which Stanley supported.

As to Westminster School, for which the Dean and Chapter were entirely responsible – though not for long, a radical change was soon to be effected by Act of Parliament in its constitution. A new Governing Body was to be set up, with the Dean as ex-officio Chairman and the Dean and Chapter empowered to appoint two persons to represent it. Westminster School was to be given the usufruct of certain properties hitherto vested solely in the Dean and Chapter and the full ownership of others. The Act of Parliament went forward and the Dean and Chapter were unable to prevent Ashburnham House, the finest private residence in the Precincts, passing out of their hands to the School. This and other exchanges of properties must have put Stanley in an embarrassing position. Every Dean of Westminster, since the Act, wears two hats, one as Chairman of Chapter, the other as Chairman of the Governing Body. This presents problems, particularly if their interests should conflict, as could happen. Having to tackle two such contentious issues so early in his reign did not prove easy for Stanley. However, he was to find across the years that the Abbey, by reason of its venerable past and independent status

as a Royal Peculiar, was able to give him unique opportunities for discharging a ministry suited to his interests and temperament. In this national church situated in the metropolis of London, Stanley, a man of wide interests, found much scope for indulging his talents.

Fortunately the Collegiate Church was sufficiently malleable and the powers attached to the office of Dean sufficiently extensive for him to inject into it his own 'style' and realize what in his opinion such a church ought to be. Stanley did not invent an alien role for Westminster Abbey, but, taking it as it was, he enlarged its scope and in doing so gave it a new momentum, *éclat* and distinction. It was to prove a ministry shot through with a welcoming liberality, placing its emphasis, as did Arnold, on a practical Christianity.

Stanley had only been at the Abbey for some four years when he produced his *Memorials of Westminster Abbey*, following up a similar work he published about Canterbury while a canon of that cathedral (1854). The *Memorials*, though it relies mainly on chronicles and memoirs instead of original sources, is a fascinating book and will always hold a unique place in the affections of those who love the Abbey. The amount of information packed into its pages, not least in its footnotes, is amazing. In the same way as Macaulay's masterpiece, his *History of England*, was a Whig document, so the *Memorials* are instinct with the kind of liberalism for which Stanley stood. The emphasis throughout is on a church which has identified itself with a nation in the varying aspects of its corporate life.

Stanley always found great satisfaction in the fact that the oath which he took on taking office pledged him to promote the 'enlargement' of the Christian Church. The Church of England's connection with the state, he believed, helped him in this endeavour, redeeming it from sectarianism, and standing for comprehensiveness. The theme of 'enlargement' thus runs throughout his sermons, his speeches and writing. That this upset critics both High and Low Church is undoubted since they tended to see it as woolly, fading off into indifferentism. On the other hand what they disliked gave great satisfaction to Nonconformists and Free Churchmen; also to such as Queen Victoria and her intelligent, liberal-minded daughter, Vicky. Thus Prothero, Stanley's biographer, writes:

In Westminster Abbey he found the material embodiment of his ideal of a comprehensive national church, an outward symbol of harmonious, unity in diversity, a temple of silence [*sic*] and reconciliation which gathered under one consecrated roof every variety of creed and every form of national activity, whether lay or ecclesiastical, religious or secular. It was one of the objects of his life to open the Abbey pulpit to churchmen of every shade of opinion, to give to laymen and ministers of other communions opportunities of speaking within its walls, to make its services attractive to all classes and all ages, to communicate to the public generally his own enthusiasm for its historical associations by conducting parties over the building, as well as compiling his *Memorials of Westminster Abbey*.

In his sermons Stanley constantly insisted that the essence of Christianity lay not in doctrinal affirmations but in a good life flowing from God's grace and manifested in Christian character. His concern was always to penetrate to the moral and spiritual experience lying behind formal doctrines which alone gave reality to institutions which embodied them. This was the basic conviction on which he founded his teaching, believing that this constituted the common ground on which Anglicans, Roman Catholics, Presbyterians, and Nonconformists could meet.

It was this liberality, this respect for an underlying unity beyond differences – though he never systematically worked out its implications – which gave point and significance to his wide-ranging travels and the books which resulted from them. Here he could see and investigate at first hand variety of race and culture underlying a common human condition. 'If you prick us, do we not bleed?' In January 1874 the Dean, accompanied by Lady Augusta, made an exciting trip to St Petersburg, representing the Queen, and participated at the marriage ceremony of the Duke of Edinburgh and the Grand Duchess Marie Alexandrovna, only daughter of Alexander II, Tsar of Russia. They were palatially, even royally, housed and Lady Augusta has left a lively and percipient account of her visit.

Not everyone, as we have seen, either at the Abbey or outside it, warmed to Stanley's embracing vision. Pusey, Liddon and Keble all felt bound to reject the Dean's invitation to preach because he had invited to the Abbey pulpit F.D. Maurice (who had been asked to resign his professorship by the Council of King's College on his publication of

Edmund Crouchback, Earl of Lancaster and son of Henry III, assisted at the translation of the body of Edward the Confessor to the High Altar in the Abbey and was a crusader in Palestine. His elaborate tomb was probably designed by Master Alexander of Abingdon.

Theological Essays in 1853) and Benjamin Jowett (suspect as a contributor to *Essays and Reviews*, 1860). One of the features of Stanley's years at the Abbey was his missionary lectures which were often delivered by laymen, for example by Max Müller, first Professor of Comparative Philology at Oxford. It was Stanley who fostered on a more considerable scale than hitherto what are called 'Special Services'. Thus he let it be known widely that he would gladly receive institutions of national importance who wished to celebrate a significant anniversary in the Abbey. He also auth-orized a performance of Bach's *St Matthew Passion*, maybe as a 'counter' to would-be High Church devotions on Maundy Thursday.

He was particularly pleased when he success-fully negotiated the return to the altar in Henry VII's Chapel of two supporting columns which had been for some time at the entrance to the Ash-molean Museum at Oxford. He was also interested in the reredos behind the High Altar placed there in 1867 and designed by Sir George Gilbert Scott.

I think it was Oscar Wilde who confessed to resisting everything but temptation. One tempt-ation, a compulsive one, Stanley decided he could not resist. With the permission of the Visitor he investigated the crypt under Henry VII's Chapel which is entered at its north-west end and drew up a detailed plan of the coffins, mostly royal, which he found there. As George III died at Windsor in his eighty-second year on 29 January 1820, having been mentally deranged over a long period, he was buried on 16 February 1820 in St George's Chapel. This has served as a precedent ever since, for all sovereigns have subsequently been buried at Windsor. So far as I know, the crypt under Henry VII's Chapel has not been 'invaded' since Stanley until it was necessary to enter the Stuart Vault in the late seventies because of a suspected leakage of natural gas. There, Charles II, William and Mary, and Queen Anne with her husband and five of her children are interred.

Later in the year of the visit to St Petersburg, Lady Augusta fell seriously ill and it was at her bedside that Stanley wrote the third section of his *Lectures on the Church*. After months of suffering during which she was visited by the Queen, she died on Ash Wednesday 1876 in the Islip wing in the Deanery. The shock to her husband was overwhelming and he never really recovered from it, though he was to live for another five years which he spent in constant activity. During the summer of 1881 he preached a series of sermons on the Beatitudes at Evensong on Saturday after-noons in the course of which he contracted erysipelas and on Saturday 9 July walked straight from the pulpit to his bed. He died on Monday, 18 July, and a week later he was buried in Westmin-ster Abbey by the side of his wife. On his tomb there is his recumbent effigy.

Never was a marriage more happy and fulfilled. Never was a relationship more outgoing in love and understanding.

Two weepers from the tomb of Edward III, these representing two of his children, the Black Prince and Joan of the Tower.

ELEVEN

'No Man is an Island, Entire of It Self'

THE DANGER with all institutions, secular or religious, is that they can too easily fall victim to an introverted myopia, preoccupied with their own domestic life and supposed interests. Yet, paradoxically, if they are to overcome this almost inevitable temptation, thereby breaking through into a wider world, they must have a firm base from which to leap over the wall; and the condition of a firm base is good human relations.

Westminster Abbey is fortunate in having at its very heart a closely knit community of clergy and laity, old and young, who bring up their families in the Precincts. It is still too male orientated, but things are moving at last. If everybody connected with the Abbey were commuters, the 'feel' of its society would be radically different. The lack of domesticity, of intimacies (and gossip) would be an impoverishment. Much must depend on the quality of life realized here.

The Abbey, which has no diocese to look to, has, fortunately, an outreach to many societies and institutions too numerous to list. In Little Cloister there resides the Rector of St Margaret's, a church closely associated over the centuries with the House of Commons. When, as is often the case, the Speaker appoints the Rector as his Chaplain, relations with members of Parliament become more personal and intimate. Along Victoria Street is the City Hall where there presides the Lord Mayor who belongs to the Abbey community as Deputy High Steward thus serving to link up the Collegiate Church with the Local Authority. A matter of yards from the Precincts are the headquarters of three great institutions – the Civil and Mechanical Engineers and the Surveyors. The Abbey has links with all these. Then there is the Methodist Central Hall and, down Victoria Street, visible now through the creation of a fine piazza, the Roman Catholic Cathedral. Our three communities have not only prayed but worked together and enjoyed the stimulus of each other's company. Nor must we forget the Abbey parishes of which the Dean and Chapter are sole or joint patrons, many of these once owned by the Abbey and regularly visited by the Abbot and monks. This still happens today and gives Abbey personnel a vivid picture of the life of the parish priest who is in the front line and absolutely essential to the ministry of the Church of England. The Royal Peculiar also has a unique connection with the Commonwealth, most of whose countries have held services here to mark their independence.

Abbey clergy and laity, when not at home in the Precincts, are often out and about serving on Commissions, giving lectures, preaching or writing books, seeking both to expound and give a rationale for Christian faith. In the last century Archbishop Tait made an effort, but unsuccessfully, to use the Dean and Chapter of Westminster as 'think tanks'. Early this century Charles Gore and William Temple were living in Little Cloister where they were busily engaged in writing works, both social and theological.

No one, in its early days, could possibly have foreseen the way a providential history would shape the Abbey's continuing life. Many questions, of a speculative, often useless kind – the 'ifs' of history – thrust themselves up. For example, what would have happened to the Abbey if the Reformation had gone the way that Sir Thomas More (and Erasmus) had wished? Would the monastery in some form or another have survived? Or again, if Oliver Cromwell's Commonwealth had survived, how would things have gone with Westminster Abbey?

As to the future? One thing we do know is that it is unpredictable. Beggars may well ride if wishes were horses but in spite of this warning let *me* indulge a wish: I like to think that in our multi-

Here the medieval monks had their lavabo; the door on the left leads to the Song School through which the Choir processes into the Abbey daily; the West Cloister is approached through the gates on the right where many organists and masters of the choristers are buried and memorialized; and then past the old trolley, the Porter's Lodge and the entrance to the Deanery and Dean's Yard.

cultural, multi-religious and multi-racial world the Abbey, without losing its distinctive Christian cutting edge, will increasingly become a host church for which its history, tradition and present standing make it ideal. How magnificent it would

be if the rich variety of faith and feeling in our contemporary world could find a home here in this Collegiate Church situated in the heart of a great metropolis.

Luther King had a dream and it is coming true. Why not this one?

Little Cloister was part of the old Infirmary. The fountain never ceases to attract, and the sound of running water in the centre of London is music indeed. There is no need to say : 'Weep you no more, sad fountains'.

*The 'incomparable' Chapter House (*RIGHT*) where the monks met to govern the Monastery until it was taken over by the House of Commons. It has not yet been returned.*

Index

References to illustrations are given in *italic* type

Abbott, Eric, 48, 53, 99
Addison, Joseph, 97
Adenauer, Konrad, 12
Alexander III, Pope, 18
Alexander of Abingdon, Master, 118
Alternative Service Book, 48–9
Ampleforth, 56, 67, 69
Amulree, 2nd Baron, 61
Andrewes, Lancelot, 50, 72, 75
Anne, Queen, 88, 118
Anne of Bohemia, Queen, *105*
Anselm, St, Archbishop of Canterbury, 59
Arbuthnot, John, 88
Arnold, Thomas, 115, 117
Ashburnham House, 117
Asquith, H. H. (*later* 1st Earl), 92
Atterbury, Francis, 50, 88, 111
Auditor, 69
Aylesbury, 2nd Earl of, 87

Bach, J. S.: *St Matthew Passion*, 44, 118
Bacon, Francis, 78
Bancroft, Richard, Archbishop of Canterbury, 72
Barnby, Sir Joseph, 44
Bates, Joah, 43
Bath, Order of the, 84
Bayeux Tapestry, 22
Beaufort, Lady Margaret, 70, 101, *101*
Beaumont, Francis, 97
Bec (Benedictine house), 59
Benedictine Order, 52, 56, 69, 70
Bennett, Rev. Joyce M., 53
Betterton, Thomas, 101
Beverley Minster, 31
Bevin, Ernest, 49
Bill, William, 71
Bishop, Henry, 84
Blake, William, 101
Blore, Edward, 12, 114
Blow, John, 40
Bonner, Edmund, Bishop of London, 85
Bourchier, Sir Humphrey, 45
Booth, General William, 104
Bridge, Sir Frederick, 41
British Broadcasting Corporation, *93*, 95
Britten, Benjamin: *War Requiem*, 44
Bromley, Sir Thomas, *50–1*
Buckingham, 1st Duke of, 78, *103*
Buckland, Mary, 113, 115
Buckland, William, 50, 110; life and career, 113–15
Burghley, 1st Baron, 71–2, 98

Busby, Richard, 90
Byrd, William, 40
Byron, George Gordon, Lord, 98

Camden, William, 74
Canning, Stratford, 100
Canterbury, 26; and Abbey's jurisdiction, 52–3
Carlyle, Thomas, 90
Caroe, Sir Olaf, 93
Chantrey, Sir Francis L., 103
Chapter House, 12, 23, *57*, 61, *123*
Chapter Office, Dean's Yard, *61*
Charles I, King, 75, 78–9, 80, 85, 90, 103
Charles II, King, 37, 40, 81, 85–7, 118
Charles Edward Stuart, Prince, 87, 95
Charles, Archdeacon, 50
Chaucer, Geoffrey, 99
Chiswick Manor, 73, 75
Choir, 12, *13*, 41, 43, 78
Choral Foundation, 40–1, 43
Christopher, St: wall painting of, 103
Church Commissioners, 117
Churchill, Sir Winston, 95, 104
Church of England (*Ecclesia Anglicana*), 37, 67; and state, 117
Clarendon, Edward Hyde, 1st Earl of, 103
Clock *see* North West Tower
Cloisters, *47*, 59
Cochrane, Admiral Thomas, 104
Coggan, Donald, Archbishop of Canterbury, 53
'College', *42*
Common Prayer, Book of *see* Prayer Book
Commonwealth (17th century), 75, 81, 86, 120
Commonwealth, British, 93–4, 120
Commonwealth Inter Faith Observance, 53
Compton, Henry, Bishop of London, 87
Cornwall, Earl of *see* John of Eltham
Coronation Appeal, 1953, 33
Coronation Chair, *89*
coronations, 81, *82*, 83–96
Cosmati floor, 27
Coward, Sir Noel, 101–2
Cowley, Abraham, 98
Cowper, William, 17
Cranmer, Thomas, Archbishop of Canterbury, 36–7, 40, 84
Cretton, Roger, 59
Crispin, Gilbert, 59, 63, 73
Croft, William, 40
Cromwell, Oliver, 75, 81, 84–6, 120
Crossing, *11*, 12–13, *106*
Customary of 1266, 37

Dark Cloister (Kill-Canon-Corner), *58*
Darwin, Charles, 12, 113
Daubeny, Giles, 1st Baron, *48*
Davidson, Randall, Archbishop of Canterbury, 92
Dean: under Statutes, 71–3
Deanery, *111*
Dean's Yard, *17*
Dimbleby, Richard, 95
Disraeli, Benjamin, 99, 100
Doddington-with-Thorpe (Lincs.), 59
Don, Alan, 53, 69, 84, 86
Donne, John, 98
Dowding, Air Chief Marshal Hugh, 1st Baron, 104
Dunstan, St, Archbishop of Canterbury, 18, 83
Dykes Bower, Stephen, 22, 26, 31
Dymoke, Dame Margery, of Ludlow, 84

Easton, Hugh, 67, 104
Ecclesia Anglicana *see* Church of England
Edgar, King of the English, 83
Edinburgh, Alfred, Duke of, 118
Edinburgh, Philip, Duke of *see* Philip
Edith, Queen of Edward the Confessor, 18
Edward, St (the Confessor), 12–13, 16, 18, 22–3, 36, *105*; shrine, *18–19*, *25*, 26–7, 30, 99; depicted on screen, 27, 30; Chapel, 72
Edward I, King, 23, 28, 62, 84, 89
Edward II, King, 84
Edward III, King, 97, *119*
Edward IV, King, 45
Edward V, King, 84
Edward VI, King, 26, 37, 84
Edward VII, King (*formerly* Prince of Wales), 41, 91, 116
Edward VIII, King (Duke of Windsor), 84, 92, 95
Edward the Black Prince, 97, *119*
Edward (Keeper of the Works), 23
Eleanor, Queen of Edward I, 36, 84, *85*
Elizabeth I, Queen, 33, 37, 44, 52, 56, 69–71, *71*, 85, 101
Elizabeth II, Queen, 92–6
Elizabeth, Queen of George VI, 92
Ely: Presbytery, 23
Epstein, Jacob, 101
Erasmus, Desiderius, 101, 120
Essex, 2nd Earl of, 75
Eastney, Abbot, 63
European Economic Community, 13
Exeter, Thomas Cecil, 1st Earl of, *98*

Fascet, George, 63

Feckenham, John, 67
Filmer, Sir Robert, 87
Fisher, Geoffrey, Archbishop of
  Canterbury, 92–6
Fox, Adam, 84
Fuller, Thomas, 67
Fulwell, John, 66

Garrick, David, 101
Gay, John, 103
Geoffrey, Abbot of Jumièges, 22, 58
George I, King, 88
George III, King, 43, 88, 90, 95
George IV, King, 89
George V, King, 12, 41, 92
George VI, King, 92, 96
Gibbons, Christopher, 40
Gibbons, Orlando, 40, 43
Gladstone, William Ewart, 100
Gloucester College, Oxford, 36
Godolphin, Charles & Mrs, 104
Godwin, Earl, 18
Goodman, Gabriel, 71–3, 73, 75
Gorbachov, Mikhail, 12
Gore, Charles, Bishop of Oxford, 50, 120
Gothic style, 21, 23, 26
Gray, Thomas, 126
guide dogs for the blind: service, 55

Habgood, John S., Archbishop of York,
  105
Hacket, John, 78
Halifax, 1st Earl of, 97
Hall, R. O., Bishop of Hong Kong, 53
Halley, Edmond, 101
Hampden, Renn Dickson, Bishop of
  Hereford, 115
Handel, George Frederick, 43; 1784
  centenary, 43
Hardyman, John, 72
Hare, Richard, 98
Harold Godwinson, King, 18, 83
Harwden, Abbot, 27
Hassall, Christopher: Out of the
  Whirlwind, 96
Hastings, Battle of, 1066, 18
Hastings, Lady Elizabeth, 1
Hawksmoor, Nicholas, 31, 42
Haydn, Joseph, 43
Hebron, Tom, 12
Henrietta Maria, Queen of Charles I,
  78, 80
Henry III, King, 12–13, 18, 22–3, 26–7,
  28, 52, 62, 99
Henry IV (of Lancaster), King, 62, 84, 105
Henry V, King, 27, 36, 46, 63, 84;
  Chantry Chapel, 13, 15, 27, 30
Henry VII, King, 29, 30, 63, 84, 101;
  Chapel, 16, 29, 30, 32, 33, 37, 55, 63,
  91, 116, 118

Henry VIII, King, 26, 52, 56, 63, 66–7, 84
Henry de Reyns, 26
Henson, H. H., Bishop of Durham, 50
Herschel, Sir John & Sir William, 101
Heylin, Peter, 78, 81, 86
Hildyard, Christopher, 48
Hill, Jane, 94
Holles, Francis, 79
Holmes, Rear-Admiral Charles, 107
Hope, Sir William St John, 91
Howard, Michael, 107
Hugh, Abbot, 58
Hume, Cardinal Basil, 69
Hunsdon, 1st Baron, 101, 102
Hyde, Anne, 87

Infirmarer and Infirmary, 61, 65
Inter Faith services, 53
Irving, Sir Henry, 101
Isham, Sir Justinian, 75
Islip, John, Abbot, 30, 56, 63, 66–7
Islip, Simon, Archbishop of
  Canterbury, 63, 67, 117

Jacobitism, 88
James I, King, 75, 78
James II, King, 87
James Francis Edward Stuart, Prince
  ('James III'), 88
Jaye, Thomas, 63
Jerusalem Chamber, 40, 52, 56, 80
Jerusalem Chamber Society, 50
Joan of the Tower, Princess, 119
Jocelin of Brakelond, 58
John of Eltham, Earl of Cornwall, 44
Jonson, Ben, 97, 99–100
Jowett, Benjamin, 118
Jumièges, Abbey of (Normandy), 22

Keats, John, 98, 104
Keble, John, 118
Kent, Victoria Mary Louisa, Duchess
  of, 90
Kidd, John, 110
King, Martin Luther, 122

Lady Chapel, 23
Lancaster, Edmund Crouchback, Earl
  of, 118
Landor, Walter Savage: Imaginary
  Conversations, 107–8
Lanfranc, Archbishop of Canterbury,
  59, 63
Lang, Cosmo, Archbishop of
  Canterbury, 92, 95
Lang, Matheson, 92
Langham, Cardinal Simon de, 46
Laud, William, Archbishop of
  Canterbury, 75, 78–9
lector theologiae, 50

Lennox, Margaret, Countess of, 69
Library, 73, 76, 78
Liddon, Henry Parry, 118
Lind, Jenny, 101
Litlyngton, Nicholas, 46, 56
Little Cloister, 122
liturgy, 36–7, 41, 45–6, 48
Lloyd Webber, Andrew: Requiem, 44
Lord Chancellor, 49, 53
Louis XIV, King of France: heart, 110

Macaulay, Thomas Babington, Lord,
  13, 87, 89–90, 117
McCulloch, Joseph, 53
McKie, Dr William, 43, 92, 95
Mane, William, 66
Mansfield, 1st Earl of, 103, 104
Mae Tse-tung, 36
Marie Alexandrovna, Grand Duchess, 118
Mary I, Queen, 26, 52, 56, 67, 69–70,
  72, 85
Mary II, Queen, 87, 118
Mary, Queen of Scots, 50–1, 71, 75
masons: at work, 27–8, 34
Maurice, F. D., 49, 114, 118
Max Müller, Friedrich, 118
Mayne, Very Rev. Michael, 56
Melbourne, 2nd Viscount, 90
memorials and monuments, 97–108
Meredith, Thomas, 73
Middlesex, 1st Earl of, 63
Milton, John, 88
monks: life, 39, 47, 59, 60, 61, 66–7, 121
Montaigne, George, Archbishop of
  York, 75
monuments see memorials
More, Sir Thomas, 120
Morgan, William, 73
Morrison, Sir John, 79
Muniment Room: ceiling boss, 81
Murchison, Sir Roderick, 114
music, 36, 40–1, 43, 49, 78
Musicians' Aisle, 99, 101
Mytton, Thomas, 79

Naseby, Battle of, 79
Nave: floor, 99
Neile, Richard, 75
Newell, Robert, 81
New Statesman, 95, 96
Newton, Sir Isaac, 101
Norfolk, 16th Duke of, 92, 95
Norfolk, 17th Duke of, 69
North Atlantic Treaty Organization, 105
North Front, 10, 31, 33
North West Tower: clock, 68

Oglethorpe, Owen, Bishop of Carlisle, 85
Oi, Florence Li Tim, 53, 55
Oldfield, Anne, 101

The poet Thomas Gray writes: 'Let not ambition mock their useful toil, their homely joys, and destiny obscure'. Frances, Duchess of Suffolk, was not likely to succumb to this temptation. A grand-daughter of Henry VII, the mother of noble but tragic Lady Jane Grey, she lived through Queen Mary's reign in dire poverty, and upon her being restored to favour, she died. A recumbent effigy on her tomb suggests a sad story. Her funeral service was the first to be conducted in the Abbey, according to the new Protestant rites.

'One People Oration', 50
O'Neilly, John, 27
organ loft and organists, 40
Our Lady of the Pew Chapel, 36
Owen, Wilfred, 107
Oxford, 2nd Earl of, 100
Oxford Movement, 13

Palmerston, 3rd Viscount, 116
Parker, Matthew, Archbishop of
    Canterbury, 75
Pearce, Zachary, 44–5
Pearson, John, 107
Peasgood, Osborne, 43
Peel, Sir Robert, *112*, 113
Pembroke, Aymer de Valence, Earl of,
    14, *114*
Pembroke, Mary, Countess of, 114
Pepys, Samuel, 87
Perkins, Jocelyn, 45–6, 48–9; *Sixty
    Years at Westminster Abbey*, 46
Peter, St, 18
Philip, Prince, Duke of Edinburgh, 33,
    92–3, 95
Pitt, William, the younger, 104
Plato, 36
Poet's Corner, 99–100, 104, 107–8, *109*
Pole, Cardinal Reginald, 85
Polydore Vergil, 66
Pope, Alexander, 101, 103
Prayer Book, 37, 40, 71
Priestley, J. B., 101
Prothero, Rowland Edmund, Baron
    Ernle, 117
Puddlicott, Richard, 62
Purcell, Henry, 36, 40
Puritans, 41, 72, 79, 81
Pusey, Edward Bouvier, 118
Pyx, Chamber of the, 23, *64*

Queen's Westminsters, 104

Raleigh, Sir Walter & Lady, 75
Raven, Charles, 93
Receiver, 55, 69
Richard II, King, 36, 46, 62, 84, *105*
Richmond and Lennox, Esmé, Duke of,
    86
Richmond and Lennox, Ludovic, Duke
    of, *86*
Robert, Master, of St Albans, 61
Robessart, Lewis (Lord Bourgchier), 103
Robinson, Armitage, 59
Rolle, John, Baron, 90
Roman Catholics, 69
Rowe, Nicholas, 103
Royal Air Force Chapel, 104
Royal Ballet School, 107
Runcie, Robert, Archbishop of
    Canterbury, 105
Russell, Lord John, 115
Ryle, Herbert Edward, 33
Rysbrack, John Michael, 103

St Catherine's Chapel, 59, 61, *65*
St Edmund, Monastery of, 58
St Edward's Chapel, 12, 13, 16, 72
St George's Chapel (Warrior's Chapel),
    104

St John's Cathedral, New York, 99
St Margaret's Church, 120
St Nicholas Chapel, *38*
St Paul's Cathedral, 31
St Peter, Collegiate Church of, 16, 33,
    56, 60
Sancroft, William, Archbishop of
    Canterbury, 87
sanctuary, rights of, 73
Sansom, Abbot, 58
Sarum rite, 37
Saunderson, Bess, 101
Savoy Hospital, 63
Scott, Sir George Gilbert, 118
Scott, Sir Gilbert, 10, 33, 107
Sharpe, John, Archbishop of
    Canterbury, 88
Shelley, Percy Bysshe, 98, 104
Sheridan, Richard Brinsley, 101
Shrewsbury, 5th Earl of: daughter, *41*
Simmonds, Mr Justice Gavin, 53
Smith, Adam, 114
Sophia, Electress of Hanover, 88
South, Robert, 50, 88
Spenser, Edmund, 99
Sprat, Thomas, 40, 87
Stanley, Lady Augusta, 90–1, 116, 118
Stanley, Arthur Penrhyn, Dean, 50–1,
    90–1, 110; life, career and works,
    115–18; effigy, *116*
Star Chamber, 78–9
Statesmen's Aisle, 99–101, *100*
Stigand, Archbishop of Canterbury,
    83
Stone (Kent): parish church, 26
Stone of Scone, 84, *89*
Stowe, John, 30
Strype, John, 72
Suffolk, Frances, Duchess of, *126*
Surveyor of the Fabric, 98–9
Swift, Jonathan, 88
Swinton, 1st Earl of, 94

Tait, Archibald Campbell, Archbishop
    of Canterbury, 120
Tallis, Thomas, 40, 43
Tanner, L. E., 84
television, 95
Temple, Frederick, Archbishop of
    Canterbury, 91–2
Temple, William, Archbishop of
    Canterbury, 50, 120
Tenison, Thomas, Archbishop of
    Canterbury, 88
Tennyson, Alfred, Lord, 101
Thomas, St: wall painting of, 103
Thorndike, Dame Sybil, 101
Thorney Island, 16, 18
Thynne, Lord John, 116–17
Times, The, 93
Tomkins, Giles & John, 40
Torrigiani, Pietro, 30, 101, *101*
Townson, Robert, Bishop of Salisbury,
    75
Trenchard, Marshal of the RAF
    Hugh, 1st Viscount, 104
Tunstall, Cuthbert, Bishop of Durham,
    85
Tyler, Wat, 105

Undercroft, 16, 23, *60*
Unknown Warrior, grave of, 12, 104
'Up School', *77*

Vere, Sir Francis, *74*
Vertue, Robert & William, 31
Vicars, John, 41
Victoria, Queen, 90–1, 99, 100, 116–17
Victoria, Princess (*later* Empress of
    Germany), 117
Visitor, 52–3
Vitalis, Abbot of Bernay, 59

Walpole, Horace, 13, 88
Walsingham, 26
Walter de Wenlok, 59, 62
Ward, W. G., 115
Ware, Abbot, 27
Warham, William, Archbishop of
    Canterbury, 67
Warren, Elizabeth, 107, *108*
Warren, John, Bishop of Bangor, 107
Warren, Max, 53
Watt, James, 103
Weelkes, Thomas, 40
Wells, H. G., 41
Wenlok, Abbot *see* Walter de Wenlok
Wesley, John, 45
Western Towers, 33, *35*
Westminster Abbey: described, 9–16;
    founded, 18; design and
    construction, 22–3, *24*, 26, 30–1, 33;
    financial dependence and appeals, 33,
    44, 55; repairs and restoration, 27–8,
    33, *34*, 67; 1560 Charter and
    Statutes, 37, 44, 56, 70, 72; offices,
    36–7, 50; 900th anniversary, 49;
    special services, 49–50, 53; acoustics,
    51; jurisdiction and independence as
    'Royal Peculiar', 52–3, 55, 73;
    Supplemental Charter, 53;
    organization of community and
    administration, 56–62, 66; monastic
    life, 59, 61–2, 67; 1303 robbery, 62;
    reconstituted under Henry VIII, 67;
    under Commonwealth, 81; new
    governing body, 117; financial
    problems, 117
Westminster Abbey Trust, 33
Westminster Cathedral, 69, 120
Westminster School, 56, 70, 73, 75, 78,
    88, 117
Wilberforce, Samuel, Bishop of
    Oxford, 113
Wilde, Oscar, 118
William I (the Conqueror), King, 18,
    58, 63, 83–4, 105
William III (of Orange), King, 40, 87, 118
William IV, King, 89–90
William of Colchester, *46*
William of Malmesbury, 22
William the Swineherd, 26
William, Austen, 53
Williams, John, 75–6, 78–9, 80–1
Wolsey, Cardinal Thomas, 66–7
Wordsworth, Christopher, 116
Wordsworth, Mary, 71
Wren, Sir Christopher, 9, 31, 33, 42

York, Philippa, Duchess of, *52–3*